HOLY
UNHAPPINESS

HOLY UNHAPPINESS

God, Goodness, and the Myth of the Blessed Life

AMANDA HELD OPELT

New York • Nashville

Worthy
Hachette Book Group
1290 Avenue of the Americas, New York, NY 10104
worthypublishing.com
twitter.com/worthypub

First Edition: July 2023

Worthy is a division of Hachette Book Group, Inc. The Worthy name and logo are trademarks of Hachette Book Group, Inc.

The publisher is not responsible for websites (or their content) that are not owned by the publisher.

The Hachette Speakers Bureau provides a wide range of authors for speaking events. To find out more, go to hachettespeakersbureau.com or email HachetteSpeakers@ hbgusa.com.

Worthy Books may be purchased in bulk for business, educational, or promotional use. For information, please contact your local bookseller or the Hachette Book Group Special Markets Department at special.markets@hbgusa.com.

Unless otherwise noted, Scripture quotations are from the Holy Bible, New International Version®, NIV® Copyright ©1973, 1978, 1984, 2011 by Biblica, Inc.® Used by permission. All rights reserved worldwide.

Scripture quotations marked ESV are from the Holy Bible, English Standard Version. ESV® Text Edition: 2016. Copyright © 2001 by Crossway Bibles, a publishing ministry of Good News Publishers.

Scripture quotations marked NKJV are from the New King James Version®. Copyright © 1982 by Thomas Nelson. Used by permission. All rights reserved.

Library of Congress Cataloging-in-Publication Data has been applied for.

ISBNs: 9781546001928 (hardcover), 9781546001942 (ebook)

Printed in the United States of America

LSC-C

Printing 1, 2023

For Tim

CONTENTS

Small is the gate and narrow the road
that leads to life, and only a few find it.

—Matthew 7:14

Is it so evident that happiness, of whatever kind,
is the only aim of mankind? If it were so,
our course would be narrow indeed,
and our destination far from elevated.

—Benjamin Constant

HOLY
UNHAPPINESS

INTRODUCTION

I am a reluctant memoirist. I'm not sure the world really needs another privileged person like me telling her story and touting advice. There's something inherently suspicious about a woman who has a solid roof over her head, food on her table, two healthy kids, and a really nice husband writing a book about unhappiness.

I've heard it said that authors will often write the book they want to read—the book they need but that doesn't yet exist. The great mystery, though, is why a person like me would feel the need for a book about unhappiness. My life, in many ways, is a picture of blessedness. It has been from the beginning.

I was born in the Bible Belt, raised in a middle-class family of four. Mine was a stable and trauma-free household of Jesus-loving people. We weren't rich, but we always had everything we needed. My parents are some of the most gracious and thoughtful people I've ever known. I was surrounded by kindness, a strong community, and plenty of opportunities to make a good start in life. I was surrounded by love.

My life has been marked not only by blessing, but also by good behavior. The path I've walked is one well worn by many people of faith who have gone before me. I grew up, went to an evangelical Christian college, and married a nice Christian boy just like my mother told me to. Having always been taught that service to others was important and admirable, I've spent the last fifteen years working in various ministries at home in the US and abroad. For the most part, I've made good decisions—grown into a responsible human adult. I followed the blueprint I was given, and I don't regret it. Some might even say I am a good person, a godly person. I do nice things for people. I volunteer and give to charity. I go to church regularly. I recycle. My husband and I now live in a lovely little town nestled in the mountains of western North Carolina with our two small kids. We still aren't rich, but I still have everything I need.

This is not to say that I have never known hardship or failure. Like most people's lives, mine has had its ups and downs. I have experienced some losses: the sudden death of my sister, who was my only sibling; a season of infertility; a health challenge or two. I still carry deep pain from these losses, still have many days when I move through the world as a mourner.

Still, all in all, anyone looking at my life would say the scales have tipped toward blessing for me. Despite the grief I've known, I have had a good life by any reasonable standard. I am comfortable, safe, and secure. In the grand scheme of history, I enjoy unprecedented prosperity and freedom. Technically speaking, I have just about everything I've ever wanted.

Yet, I have known unhappiness. Deeply.

This book won't begin like other self-help books I've read, where the author experiences a moment of acute crisis on a yoga mat or a heartbreaking epiphany on the bathroom floor of her suburban home, sending her on a journey of self-discovery and rebirth. My unhappiness did not descend on me like some grand revelation. It has been more like a slow drip of disappointment. I've lived with it for almost as long as I can remember, but I wouldn't call it clinical anxiety or depression. The feeling is something akin to restlessness, like an ever-present anticlimax. It feels like lack, almost as if I am expecting something out of life that has not yet been delivered. Sometimes the sadness looms large, feels like a boulder I'm carrying. Sometimes it's as small as a pebble in my shoe. But it is always there, pressing painfully in at every step.

Put succinctly, I feel like *life* has let me down somehow.

I understand how off-putting this must sound. Having worked in humanitarian aid and social services, I know what real deprivation looks like, so I feel the cringeworthiness of all this even as I type it. And I feel confusion. Frankly, my feelings are a bit baffling. What could a person like me—with all the love I've been given and all the material comforts I've enjoyed—possibly have to complain about? What is it, exactly, that's bothering me so much?

Why doesn't my very, very blessed life *feel* like a blessing?

The concept of blessedness has had a long and storied history, particularly within religious circles. The prosperity gospel—a popular expression of faith within the Protestant Christian religion—has worked hard to corner the market on the #blessed life. This "gospel" emerged in the late nineteenth century as a mix-and-match doctrine of New Thought ideology and Pentecostalism. New Thought—which was a nineteenth-century spiritual movement disseminated by mesmerists, healers, and philosophers—emphasized the power of the mind to achieve success and affluence. Physical reality, its proponents taught, had its origin in the mental and metaphysical spheres. Followers of New Thought believed positive thinking could lead to wealth, and prayers for restoration could lead to health.[1] Most of today's popular self-help books are ideological descendants of this movement. Theirs is the staunch insistence that we can control our outcomes by our own efforts, self-confidence, and optimism.

After the turn of the century, New Thought began to influence some of the leadership within the Pentecostal Church, which was experiencing a series of revivals in America. Pentecostalism—with its emphasis on the individual's personal relationship with God, the baptism of the Holy Spirit, speaking in tongues, and the power of divine healing—embraced the notion that there is authority in the spoken word and power in positive thinking. Great faith can accomplish great things in our lives. Thus, the Word of Faith and prosperity movements were born.

By the mid-1900s prosperity faith healers and revivalists began asking their followers for "seed money," tithes and donations to be given to the ministry. Healers promised tithers that these funds would be returned to them by God sevenfold, thirtyfold, even a hundredfold.[2] This false promise funded the personal empires of prosperity televangelists and influencers. A series of scandals including fraud and extramarital affairs plagued the movement in the 1980s, with many of its leaders being widely criticized for their lavish and opulent lifestyles.

The prosperity gospel of today has experienced a nice recovery, with its new leaders enjoying huge sway in the world of Christian publishing and media. Many of America's megachurches are of the Word of Faith tradition, and the movement has gained huge ground in countries across Africa and Asia. While its current iteration is a bit toned down from the days of gaudy stage furniture, pink hair, and glittering promises, the core tenets remain:

God desires for you to be healthy and wealthy. You are entitled to blessing. The abundant life can be achieved through the power of positive thinking and a confident word of faith. You will *always* reap what you sow. You are capable of great things if you only believe in yourself. Suffering is a result of a negative mindset or lack of faith.[3] It is an ideology that pairs well with the modern wellness movement and situates itself nicely in the abundance of our twenty-first-century American lifestyles.

Every church I've ever been part of has rejected the prosperity gospel outright—named it a pariah within Christendom. Growing up I was taught that adversity was nothing to be feared, that poverty and sickness were to be expected. They were not a sign of failure on my part or a lack of favor on God's part. I never felt entitled to affluence and always believed that God was good even when my circumstances were not.

But despite my well-constructed theology of suffering, there are elements of the prosperity gospel's values that feel vaguely familiar to me. While I did not believe that God was a vending machine for material abundance, I did expect God to make me *happy*, to bless me spiritually and experientially. This expectation was nurtured by a million different messages, some implicit and some explicit, that I received from my community of faith. Believe the right things and you will *feel* the right way, or so the assumption goes. God may not grant me health and wealth. But most certainly, he was supposed to grant me *emotional* prosperity: fulfillment in work, meaning in ministry, intimacy with God, and purpose in suffering.

This gospel seemed way less menacing to me than a gospel that esteems money and sees illness and death as a sign of failure. But the emotional prosperity gospel is its own subtle form of heresy, a narrative woven together by threads of half-truths and plenty of proof texts. A theology that is partially true and partially false is especially insidious because it's easy to defend and difficult to denounce. You end up getting pulled along by its wise and appealing pieces and confused by the bits that don't quite square with Scripture or reality. I never thought to question it, never imagined it would lead me astray.

In many ways the ideology was "caught, not taught," as they say. This set of propositions crept its way into the language of popular Christian books, music, sermon series, and wall decor. It permeated the evangelical churches I attended. It was a sacrosanct rendition of "the good life." We weren't necessarily conscious of it, but we maintained that same sense of entitlement characteristic of the health and wealth gospel. God wants to bless me. *God wants to make me happy.* Make good choices and peace will be the norm and pain an aberration. There were divine reciprocities that were mine to be had:

Get a good job, and you'll be happy.

Marry and have lots of kids, and you'll be happy.

Discover God's will for your life, and you'll be happy.

Grow close to God, and you'll be happy.

I was living in the shadow of this cosmic equation, this intoxicating formula for what the good life would look like: If this, then that. Give this, and you'll receive that; sow this and you'll reap that. Cause and effect. My seed money was my theological acumen, my good behavior, and my good choices. And the return on investment would be deep, abiding joy.

More than a decade ago, when I was a newlywed struggling with marriage, work, and ministry, I was having coffee with my friend Reva. We were talking about how surprisingly difficult marriage can be and I said to her through tears, "I just feel like a failure… like something is wrong with me!"

Reva, with her dark, earnest eyes and pensive smile, replied back: "Or maybe it's not you at all! Maybe there's something wrong with the *system*, Amanda." Her voice trembled a bit, brimming with both compassion for me and contempt for said system. Reva is very smart, so I figured she knew what she was talking about. I nodded vigorously back at her. "Yeah!" I exclaimed in reply. "Totally! The system is *so* messed up!"

Honestly, though, I had no idea what she meant by "the system." I remember nervously thinking to myself, *Um…what system?* But instead of asking her to explain more, I just wiped the tears from my eyes, took another gulp of coffee, and the conversation moved on.

Looking back, I think I now understand what Reva meant. I'm realizing that every category of our lives—whether it's work or marriage or friendship—has a system associated with it, a set of assumptions and underlying beliefs that inform our experiences and expectations. Some of these beliefs grew from philosophical, theological, and sociological developments that find their roots far back in history. It's wild how a famine, plague, war, technological innovation, political crisis, or religious awakening that occurred centuries before our lifetimes can shape a society's mindset for years to come. Our longings, our tendencies, our inclinations, and our definitions of "good" and "bad" are not born out of thin air. For all our claims of individualism, freedom of feeling, and autonomy of thought, there are forces at work outside of us that have built the mental and psychological scaffolding of our lives.

Before I tell you what this book *is*, I will tell you what it *is not*. It is not a comprehensive inquiry into these historical and philosophical forces. It is not an exhaustive theological analysis of what it means biblically to flourish or to be blessed. I won't exactly be presenting you with a thesis. I don't claim to have found the secret to true happiness, and I won't be leaving you with a ten-step program that will lead to a life of blessing.

This book is simply my story. It is an account of what it was like to encounter sadness in my shoes, as a female, millennial, white, American Christian. I recognize that no one person's experience of modern America is exactly the same. Moreover, Christianity in America—even *evangelical* Christianity in America—is not a monolith. But this is *my* experience. And my gut tells me that if you've picked up this book, you'll recognize some of your own story in mine.

I've written about nine facets of life that I believe have been tainted by the emotional prosperity gospel. These are the down payments we make on happiness, the "if this, then that" conditions and assurances we embrace as trustworthy and true. I'll explore the myths we believe about these areas of life and the ways we've idolized them as mechanisms for meaning and fulfillment. I'll examine the choices we make and the expectations that come with those choices. I'll be looking not only at my own expectations, but also at society's expectations and, more specifically, the Church's expectations. So yes, you will find a little bit of history here—and some theology too. But I am writing this book very much as a learner, as someone who is still in process. At its core this book is the story of the disappointment—and sometimes shock—I felt when none of these facets of life consistently delivered the psychological outcomes I expected. You may find that the words meander a bit, as words are prone to do when we are trying to make sense of an experience.

And so, it is with a healthy dose of humility that I will also share three ways I am learning to reimagine goodness. These are not prescriptive blessings, but they are descriptive of what I found to be the backbone of *true* happiness once some of those myths and excesses melted away. You'll find those reflections at the end of each section of the book. My hope is that I am slowly learning to trade my expectations of "the good life" for a deeper form of goodness—blessings that are simpler but sturdier. More durable.

No doubt, my deepest conviction will likely rise to the surface throughout: I no longer believe that my sadness makes me a failure, that my restlessness means there is something wrong with me. The notion that if I am *good* then my experiences and my feelings will always be *good* is a myth. Life is hard no matter how many good choices you make. People die and disasters befall us, certainly. But there is deep pain even in the small, daily afflictions: Work is wearisome, relationships are frustrating, our resolve is finite, and our optimism fails. Even our "blessings" come with a cost. Despite our faithfulness to all the spiritual disciplines, God can sometimes feel achingly absent. Life often demands more of us than we know how to give. We are not as strong as our circumstances require us to be. Simply being human is a rigorous endeavor.

But no one really wants *that* hand-lettered and hanging on their wall.

What exactly is "the good life"? What does it mean to be happy?

These are the questions, of course, that troubled me when I first began writing this book. Humans have struggled to define happiness since the dawn of time. In the course of my study, I learned that for the ancient Greeks, happiness was not so much a subjective feeling experienced in the moment, but rather the characterization of an entire life—one of honorable achievements, familial health, and public esteem. Happiness can be measured only at the end of one's life when all things have been considered. While virtue has always been associated with the concept of "the good life," for most of human history, happiness was thought to be primarily the result of luck, fate, or a gracious act of the gods.[4] A mere human couldn't hope to achieve happiness for himself, no matter his virtue. Likewise, prolonged sadness, or *melancholia*, was believed to be an unlucky imbalance of the *humours*, or bodily fluids.[5]

Even our language is evidence of this perceived lack of agency. When the Greeks spoke of happiness, they often used the noun *eudaimonia*, comprising the Greek *eu* (good) and *daimon* (god, spirit, or demon), indicating that the good life was in the hands of unseen benevolent—or malevolent—spiritual beings. The root of our English word "happiness" comes from the Middle English and Old Norse *happ*, which means "chance" or "fortune." Words like "haphazard," "hapless," and "perhaps" all find their origin in this term. The French word for happiness is *bonheur*, derived from *bon* (good) and *heur* (luck). Romance languages draw their words for happiness from the Latin *felix*, which means "fate" or "luck."[6]

It was only during the age of Enlightenment—with its emphasis on reason, individual freedom, and human rights—that our modern conceptions of happiness began to truly take shape. Our American forefathers classified the "pursuit of happiness" as a self-evident, unalienable right in our government's founding documents, a sign of the changing times. And while many scholars speculate that for Thomas Jefferson, "happiness" as stated in our Declaration of Independence was likely defined more in terms of economic opportunity, material security, and social stability,[7] most Americans have come to associate happiness with a sense of deep psychological fulfillment and self-actualization. It is a feeling experienced in the moment. We believe we are entitled not just to the pursuit of it, but to the attainment of it. It is almost as if one has a duty to oneself to achieve a happy life. Happiness is no longer a matter of fate, but of personal willpower.

Americans in particular maintain a special aversion to pain and suffering. We are incredibly proficient at avoiding hurt and putting on an optimistic face. If you are an American of European descent, it means that your ancestors initially came to these shores for the very purpose of *escaping* hardship. They were fleeing persecution, poverty, and oppression. The insistence on a better tomorrow is written on our DNA.[8]

We have our own venerated and time-tested formula: Work hard, make good choices, believe in yourself, and then your dreams will come true. This commitment to personal agency is the pioneering spirit of the frontier. Americans are always moving toward new horizons, pulling ourselves up by our bootstraps through rugged self-reliance. The world's leading scholar on the history of the prosperity gospel, Kate Bowler, believes that the theology of abundance gained such a foothold within the American religious landscape because it echoes the ideals our nation has cherished since its founding. She writes:

The prosperity gospel was constituted by the deification and ritualization of the American Dream: upward mobility, accumulation, hard work, and moral fiber. If the prosperity gospel can be taken as a gauge of the nation's self-perception, this is surely a country soaring with confidence in the possibility of human transformation. The movement's culture of god-men and conquerors rang true to a nation that embraced the mythology of righteous individuals bending circumstances to their vision of the good life.[9]

It is impossible to overstate how much New Thought and the prosperity gospel have shaped the emotional landscape of this country. If positive thinking has the power to activate abundance, then negative feelings are marginalized, told they don't belong. We are a culture that has forgotten how to be sad. We don't know how to grieve or be angry. We palliate pain, and numb discomfort with drugs, entertainment, busyness, and productivity. We've marginalized unhappiness, removed it from our vocabulary. Most negative feelings have been pathologized, stigmatized, and named as being outside the realm of normal. Instead, we have normalized peace, prosperity, and positivity. We whitewash our narratives, leave out all the shameful failures of our American origin story. We close our ears to the truth. We insist on bliss. When a task or commitment or relationship becomes too emotionally difficult, we jump ship, lest the bad feelings weigh down our lives. We have a million different methods for "balancing our humours."

While Christians may claim to be more willing to suffer through and honor our commitments, we, too, have marginalized pain and sadness. Since the fourth century, "sadness"—or some version of it—has been included on the Church's various lists of significant vices, most notably the seven deadly sins. Sometimes termed "acedia," other times "sloth," the core belief was that a dejection of spirit was an affront to God.[10] Even though the early Church often venerated the *experience* of suffering as a pathway to glory, with many aspiring to martyrdom, the emotional reaction of sadness was rarely acceptable.

To this day, Christians have a way of labeling negative emotions as unholy, insinuating that difficult feelings like fear, listlessness, anger, or anxiety are the result of a lack of trust in God. More than once, I remember a preacher saying something to this effect: "God gets ahold of us through the mind and intellect, and Satan gets ahold of us through the heart and emotions." This led me to believe that emotions were not to be trusted, particularly difficult emotions. They were sinister, an indication of a poorly formed theology. Sadness is sin. Worry is wicked. Truth can tame *any* ungodly emotion.

And so, for the better part of my life, whenever I experienced difficult emotions, I'd recoil. I'd feel shame. I'd think of myself as a failure. I'd run through a script of pithy pious statements to try to convince everyone, including myself, that I was fine. I was *just fine*. I'd prove my holiness by demonstrating my happiness.

I'm too blessed to be stressed.

God won't give me more than I can handle.

Everything happens for a reason.

I should just let go and let God.

Pray more; worry less.

Faith over fear.

Somewhere along the way, these statements stopped being enough. I was no longer able to pretend I was okay. My sadness was getting the better of me. The formula had broken down. I was lost. My evangelical upbringing had prepared me for the concept of suffering, but not for the actual experience of it.

The reason I overcame my memoirist impostor syndrome and ultimately decided to write this book was because I know I'm not alone. Almost every day, I meet fellow humans, and even fellow believers, who have that look of having been hoodwinked. They've made all the right decisions and done all the right things, and still, life *feels* hard for them. I wrote the book *I* needed to read because I'm certain there's at least one other person out there who needs these words as much as I do.

In this book, I make an attempt to befriend my sorrow rather than begrudge it. I've decided that my sadness has something to say, and my discomfort has something to teach me about myself, about God, and about the world around me. And though I have tried to reimagine what it truly means to be blessed, you won't find the familiar "blessing in disguise" trope here. You'll soon discover I'm not wild about the concept of silver linings, and I don't like being pressured to always find a purpose for my pain.

This is a book for people who are curious about their discontent, for people who are tired of numbing and ready to feel, for people who are willing to normalize sorrow and rescue it from the margins. It is a book that investigates the cost of our commitment to optimism, and tries to understand if there is a blessedness to be found beyond our sacred formulas, positive feelings, and saccharine sentiments. This is a book for people who think that perhaps there is holiness to be found in their unhappiness.

HOLY
UNHAPPINESS

PART 1

CHAPTER 1

WORK
(Get a Good Job)

God is a gardener.

I feel this truth deep in my bones every year in May, when I climb the steep hill behind our house to our small garden patch, where in the past five years we have successfully grown approximately three green peppers, a small handful of strawberries, nine or ten cherry tomatoes, and one enormous zucchini.

The Appalachians are an inhospitable place for a garden. The growing season is short at our elevation and frequent rainfall stunts growth. The soil is rocky, and flat bottomland is scarce. Every year, we are faced with some new weather-related disaster—a freak snowfall in May, a flood, a hailstorm, an early frost. The wildlife is antagonistic. As if being summoned to a casting call for a Disney movie, woodland creatures great and small make their annual descent upon our small patch of vegetables—rabbits, moles, squirrels, deer, chipmunks, black bears, blue jays, and sparrows. Bounty is a concept we are unfamiliar with. The carrots are typically uprooted, the tomatoes blighted, the squash tough, the kale pockmarked by hungry beetles.

Hermann Buhl once said, "Mountains have a way of dealing with overconfidence."[1] Here in the highlands, you can step into an endeavor with all the hope in the world, inspired by visions of vitamin-rich veggie pastas, piled-high salad plates, tangy salsas, and luxurious berry pies. It doesn't take long for those hopes to be disappointed, your energy depleted, your efforts seemingly wasted.

But for my husband, Tim, this annual humiliation is nothing to be feared. He comes from a long line of Wisconsin dairy farmers. His hopefulness is as hardy as his work ethic. Typical of many Midwesterners, he seems to have a short-term memory when it comes to agronomical failure. His posture is one of steady resolve. He is deeply committed to the notion that work, in and of itself, is good—enjoyable even. No matter the outcome, Tim believes it is healthy to set your hand to a task, to sweat, to feel the strain of muscle for a cause you believe in.

Tim seems to have embraced with his heart and his hands a theological truth I've only ever known in my head: We were created to work. In Paradise itself, before the fall, before the curse, before sin had permeated the world with pain, we were told to cultivate a garden, and God said it was good. More than that, we were created to co-labor with God.

This was a truth embedded in the hearts of God's people, Israel, from the very beginning. In the wide array of early Mesopotamian metanarratives, Israel's origin story was an outlier, her God an anomaly. Most other cultures of the ancient Near East saw labor as odious and dishonorable. Legend holds that the gods of Babylon needed food to survive, but they didn't want to be bothered with the work required to plant, grow, and harvest. So they created humans as a slave race, a menial task force to have at their disposal. In Egyptian cosmogony, where natural elements like the sky, sun, rain, and plants were all associated with divinity, humans were regarded as a wretched and lowly race. They were the only nondivine beings in all of creation, and they had the misfortune of being appointed a destiny defined by mundane and tiresome labor.[2]

But the God of Israel began telling the story of his love for humanity by casting *himself* as the laborer. The language from Genesis is beautifully anthropomorphic.[3] God speaks, names, separates, forms, breathes, and plants. He even performs surgery on an unsuspecting Adam. And then, God rests.

In this story, the man and the woman are given the roles of co-laborers and co-creators. In fact, their identity as workers is part of what makes them image bearers of God. God plants the garden, and humankind tends and keeps the garden. This was his plan from the beginning and part of the goodness of creation. Gardening is an occupation fit for God himself and is given as an honorable inheritance to his children. Work was never meant to be a curse, punishment, or the drudgery of the lowly.[4]

Work is a holy responsibility. Many scholars believe the act of tending the garden in Genesis parallels the sacred service of maintaining the temple. The image of Adam and Eve's agricultural undertaking is of a priestly nature—as if the garden itself was a sanctuary and the entire world the temple of God.[5] Here we begin to see the connection between vocation and worship, labor and liturgy. Every one of us is born into a bloodline of ancient gardener priests.

Author and activist Lisa Sharon Harper notes that part of the goodness God saw in his creation was the goodness *between* things—the ultimate state of shalom that existed in the new world[6]—where the return was equal to the investment, the joy of the labor matched the joy of the harvest, and the earth was agreeable to our sowing and reaping. Relationships were just, and flourishing was not a zero-sum game. God, whose Spirit hovered over the waters of chaos, brought order to disorder. Woman and man ruled over the earth lovingly, rejoicing in the yield, at peace with themselves, with each other, with God, and with the world.

God is a gardener, a grower of good things. And God is with me when I labor, when I cultivate his good earth. Just as I was made in the image of God, I was made to be a gardener. I was made to work.

But was I made for the disappointment, for the disillusionment that sets in when a task I've undertaken doesn't come to full fruition? What about our garden? Was I made to be met by failure, to see my efforts wasted, to feel the sting of a fruitless venture again and again? Was I made for the exhaustion, frustration, and burnout that so often accompany work in our day and age? Was I made for the defeat of all my hopes and dreams and aspirations?

I was made to plant seeds. But was I made to reap thorns and thistles?

In elementary school, when career day rolled around, I always struggled to pick out a costume. Which is to say I struggled to choose a life calling. As a young child, I dreamed of growing up and becoming a cowgirl. It took me until age six to realize that wasn't exactly a lucrative profession. I then considered more practical occupations such as gymnast, rock band frontwoman, and professional dog walker. My indecision didn't improve with age. I changed my major three times in college. My employment history could be described as erratic at worst, nomadic at best. I suppose I'm simply a product of my culture, an archetype of the meandering millennial, always in search of the next best thing. The average tenure for workers of my generation is 2.8 years.[7] Sometimes I hate that I'm so "on-brand" for someone my age. And there's nothing millennials hate more than being accused of being a millennial.

My generation is certainly unique when it comes to work. The vast majority of people throughout history have had few options when it came to vocation. Unless you were part of the upper echelon of society, your lot in life was to work your fingers to the bone, day after day, merely to survive. If your father was a fisherman, you were a fisherman. If he was a farmer, you were a farmer. Many were born into slavery or serfhood, the fruit of their labor exploited by a lord or master. Societies were stagnant, a person's station in life determined by a fixed economic stratum. There was no such thing as upward mobility or a "career move." Kids weren't taking occupational aptitude tests in high school. Actually, most kids didn't go to high school. It may be hard for affluent Westerners to wrap their minds around that level of vocational immobility, but frankly this is the condition that persists for much of the world to this day.

The rise of free market capitalism, wage labor, and industrialization in the eighteenth century initiated a significant change in the way we in the West think about work. European colonialism was in full swing at that time, and global trade was expanding significantly. For Western societies, this meant that various goods such as sugar, coffee, porcelain, pocket watches, and textiles were available to a growing market. Ordinary families may not hope to find occupations they loved or reach an entirely new socioeconomic class. But hard work and a good job could create a path to greater purchasing power and at least a modest amount of financial progress. Work was becoming a means to a material end, not simply a means of survival or the demand of a king or lord.[8] Eighteenth-century economist James Steuart noted that in former times, "men were…forced to labour because they were slaves to others; men are now forced to labour because they are slaves to their own wants."[9]

Capitalism's emphasis on greater and faster production of goods ushered in the age of division of labor. Agrarian communities moved toward industrialized cities, unwittingly creating a largely automated, machine-like labor force. Prosperity for some came at an unfathomable cost to others. The vast reach of colonialism devastated indigenous societies across the globe. While Western economies experienced unprecedented growth and goods became more accessible, working conditions in many factories were squalid, the labor of children was egregiously exploited, indentured servitude flourished, and the vile practice of chattel slavery continued largely unchecked for generations.

America survived a civil war, two world wars, and the Great Depression. And with the end of World War II came unprecedented prosperity and an ever-transforming perspective of the nature and purpose of work. My parents' generation was the first to experience the full benefits of this widespread affluence. Leading expert on multigenerational workforces Haydn Shaw notes that prior to the baby boomer era, work was predominantly associated with *sacrifice* and *survival*. Boomers' parents—sometimes referred to as the Greatest Generation—had endured the Great Depression through frugality and innovation. They had defeated global fascism and totalitarianism by sacrifice and unified cooperation. They

8

were duty-driven and knew how to be satisfied with a little. But boomers wanted more—more out of life, more out of work. In the mid-twentieth century, work became associated not with survival but rather with *self*.[10] Questions like *Do I enjoy my job? Is this work meaningful?* and *Do I like living here?* were readily asked by the boomer generation, at least in the privileged middle and upper classes. Work was not so much about making a contribution to the common good, but rather about making your own path, about doing what was right for *you* and *your* dreams.

In 1959, *Life* magazine announced, "For the first time, a civilization has reached a point where most people are no longer preoccupied with providing food and shelter."[11] Advertising through radio and television presented to boomers and Gen Xers new products that would create an ideal way to live, connecting them to a larger global marketplace and community. There was a great big world of stuff and experiences out there. And it was all within reach. *If* you could find the right job.

Global connection has only grown, with millennials emerging as the largest demographic in the workforce. While capitalism continues to run its course, many Gen Xers, millennials, and Gen Zers are less and less preoccupied with the stuff their professional earnings can buy. We are more interested in the experiences and personal meaning that can be derived from our careers. We've internalized the self-directedness inherent in consumerism and transferred it from the need for products to a need for purpose. Christian speaker and author Jefferson Bethke wrote: "Work used to be about making things. Then all of a sudden, work was about making *us*."[12]

Writer and management expert Bruce Tulgan says of professional millennials, "From the first day they arrive in the workplace, they are scrambling to keep their options open, leverage their uniqueness for all its potential value, and wrap a customized career around the customized life they are trying to build."[13] We want our jobs the way *we* want them.

As much as I hate to admit it, I am a true millennial. I always had the impression that the perfect job was out there for me, something that was suited specifically to fit my own unique gifts and interest. Finding *that* job, I was told, would forge the path to a happy life. Through that work, I could experience fulfillment, satisfaction, and a prosperity not only of provision but of purpose. I didn't just want to pay my bills. I wanted every hour I spent on the clock to be a meaningful experience.

Find that perfect job, I was told, and you will "never work a day in your life."

Ce∽

I've had my dream job. Three times.

But before I had my dream jobs, I had a job I thought was ordinary. Uninspiring. It was a landscaping gig at a historic botanical garden in Nashville called Cheekwood. I took the job one year after I graduated from college, during a season of vocational indecision. Immediately following graduation, I'd gone to work as a missionary to India where I'd quickly figured out I did not really want to be a missionary. I moved back into my parents' basement for a few months to cry and pray and figure out what was next. A friend and I decided to rent a house in Nashville together where my full-time occupation became checking the wanted ads and playing guitar in local dive bars for free pizza.

Rent was due and I needed to eat something other than pizza.

Indecision unfortunately doesn't pay the bills. Neither does open mic night. So, I did something I thought I'd never do and applied for a position in manual labor. When the human resources department at Cheekwood called me in for an interview, the only question they really asked me was, "What's your favorite flower?"

"Petunias," I said.

I was hired on the spot.

The setting of this job (a floral dreamscape) was top-notch. But the work itself was exhausting—backbreaking at times. My colleagues and I would mow and weed-eat the lawns. We would shovel mulch and spread fertilizer. We'd haul endless yards of water hoses to far-flung flower beds at the outskirts of the grounds. All this was done in the scorching heat of a Middle Tennessee summer, where some days it was ninety degrees in the shade.

One week, the park managers decided to drain a large koi pond located in the middle of the grounds in order to reseal the pond bottom, which had apparently started leaking. My teammate Steve and I were commissioned to rescue the koi fish as the pond was being drained, no easy task and a risky one, too, on account of all the snapping turtles who also lived in the pond.

Steve and I discussed our various options for this important mission and searched the supply shed for the tools we'd need. First, we tried dredging the pond with a large net that we each held at either end while teetering on the edges of the banks. But after three passes, we came up with only half a dozen koi. So, we put on waders and rubber boots, and slogged our way into the sludge of the draining pond, each with a landing net in one hand and a bucket in the other.

We spent the afternoon sloshing around and poking our nets into the muddy water. Flecks of shiny gold, white, and yellow emerged from the muck, and the koi wriggled wildly as we hurried to scoop them up. We were treasure hunters, lifting shimmering prizes from the mire. The search became more urgent the lower the water levels got. In the end, we lost some of the koi. But we were able to rescue most of them and deliver them to a temporary home until the pond was resealed and filled with water again. Steve and I left that evening covered in mud, exhausted, and sore, but feeling that priceless joy and pride that come with a job well done and an effort rewarded. That night I fell into my bed, sleep engulfing me immediately. Images of glittering scales flopped in and out of my dreams.

I know it sounds strange, but it was one of the best days of my life.

Despite the success of the koi rescue operation, I'm not particularly well suited for a career in landscaping and horticulture—as is currently evidenced by my less than successful vegetable patch. Besides that, I had a deeply embedded notion that manual labor couldn't be as honoring to God as a job in ministry or in the service sector. Digging up weeds, deadheading gardenias, and saving fish wasn't the holy, exciting work I had envisioned on career day growing up. I had my sights set on being a "fisher of men." The following fall, I was hired for my first dream job, as a program manager for a Christian nonprofit that served underemployed women in downtown Nashville. I turned in my waders and gardening gloves to the Cheekwood office. Not only was I excited to enjoy air-conditioning again, I was also eager to finally put my value of "serving the poor" into action.

My job was to manage a ministry site that provided GED tutoring, professional skills training, job searching, and community resource networking. Each participant was provided with a one-on-one mentor, childcare for their study time, and help with transportation to and from class. I coordinated all the volunteers for the ministry and worked with individual participants as they pursued their educational and employment goals.

I should have known from the koi pond that my savior complex runs deep. After I started my career in community service, I was pretty proud of myself—for the long hours I worked, for the personal sacrifices I made, for the ways I thought I was helping. But I quickly learned that generational poverty and systemic injustice cannot be put to rights by some ambitious do-gooder who thinks she can save the world all on her own. There were days that felt truly fruitless. I watched my students struggle. We rejoiced when anyone landed an entry-level job, but we all carried the heavy knowledge that minimum wage was simply not enough to live on. We threw a party when anyone passed the GED, but we knew few bosses would care enough to give a raise for that extraordinary accomplishment. There were always evictions, broken-down cars, and outrageous medical bills to contend with.

The work was hard. For every beautiful moment of meaningful connection with a student, there were mounds of paperwork and planning to do. Volunteers are wonderful. And hard to lead. Fundraising is demoralizing. Grant management requires an immense amount of data entry. The job I thought I'd always wanted—the *work*, the *service* I had always dreamed of doing—began to deplete me. I'd hoped it would feel rewarding, purposeful. Instead, it just felt like a drag.

Three years into the job, when Tim told me he was thinking

about pursuing graduate work at a university out of state, I jumped at the chance to quit without having to admit I was crumbling. I could blame my resignation on my husband, not my burnout. I wouldn't have to admit defeat—to myself, to my friends, or to God. I could slip away and thank everyone for the wonderful three years I'd had at the ministry, feigning sadness while secretly rejoicing that I was finally done.

The town we moved to for Tim's graduate work was home to an international disaster relief organization. I'm not sure why I thought a career in humanitarian aid would somehow serve as a reprieve after my grueling time in nonprofit work. But having lived in India for a short time after college, the international bug had bitten me. I had visions of traveling the world, of swooping in and providing lifesaving aid in places I had only seen on the news or in *National Geographic*. I guess that savior complex is pretty hard to shake.

It was indeed an adventure. I traveled to more than a dozen countries, serving as a staff care specialist for our international workers. The daily news headlines determined my workload, and that felt very exciting. I loved the thrill of it all, enjoyed telling my friends and family where I had been and what I had done. My passport was bulging with visas and immunization cards. My Facebook page was filled with pictures from all over the world. Most importantly, I met some of the most wonderful, courageous people you could ever imagine. Like I said, it was my dream job.

Except for when it wasn't. Being an adrenaline junkie can take quite a toll on your nervous system. I didn't love being stressed and jet-lagged all the time. And the administrative tasks required to get my work done were relentless. "Aid work ain't kissing babies," my colleagues and I would often groan to one another. We never dreamed helping victims of disasters would mean spending so much time working on Excel spreadsheets.

Looking back on my job history, I see how my privilege had created a sinister sense of self-importance. For starters, there was an inconspicuous but deeply problematic exploitation inherent in my work aspirations. My employment was based on the hardships and crises of other people. It is a noble thing to want to help those in need, but unfortunately, I sometimes failed to see the people I was helping as anything more than simply the beneficiaries of my work. Their tragedies had created for me opportunities for personal adventure, purpose, meaning, and adrenaline hits. I'd shown up for the photo op but was quickly confronted with the reality of the pain in the world. That was jarring. And when I got tired, I could clock out or resign. But for victims of injustice, warfare, and famine, the exhaustion, the trauma, and the grief continue.

Moreover, I had assumed that finding the right job, one that allowed me to serve in the name of Jesus and do work I loved, would make me happy, would always be fulfilling. I wasn't counting on the days when I was overrun with paperwork. I wasn't expecting the long meetings, the conflicts with fellow employees, the initiatives that failed, the spreadsheets that accidentally got deleted and lost in the ether. I wasn't expecting the boredom that comes from doing the same job, year after year, even if it is a job that, on paper, you love.

And so, I quit my second dream job. Burnout wasn't exactly the reason. I'd become a mom and I wanted work that was more flexible and a bit less intense. I decided to dedicate my time solely to my kids and to my writing. I wrote up a proposal for a book, and miraculously, it was accepted by a publisher.

So here I am, hunched over my computer in my home office.

I've reheated my coffee three times now. At this point, I've been at it for an hour, and I suspect there are more Cheetos in my belly than words on the page. Writing, it turns out, is hard work. I've thrown out five paragraphs for every one I've kept. Stacks of research books loom in the corner, begging to be read, but my eyelids keep drooping. I reheat my coffee again.

I'm living the dream. I get paid to write, paid to be creative. Unlike most of my ancestors, I actually got to *choose* my career. I'm among the most privileged generation in all of history. Why, then, am I still so frustrated, so tired, so agitated? Why am I not happy? Why do I sometimes daydream about returning to the backbreaking but astonishingly satisfying work of gardening? Why do I sometimes wish I could spend the rest of my life getting paid pennies to scoop shimmering fish out of the mud?

ᏟᎾᏒ

Work hard, and you'll be happy. Find a job you love, and you'll be happy. Engage in the labor of philanthropy or ministry, and you'll be happy.

These are some of the great promises of the emotional prosperity gospel. And yet the curse of Genesis 3 tells a different story. Our primordial parents whisper a somber warning to us: *The ground of your labor is cursed.*

After the beautiful and awe-inspiring creation narrative and poetry of Genesis 1 and 2, Genesis 3 is a rude awakening. In it we find ourselves at the foot of the Tree of the Knowledge of Good and Evil, where we are given a front-row seat in the unfolding of the fall. We witness the private lives of our progenitors: the clandestine schemes of a slithering serpent, the human heart's pursuit of power, the prideful blame-shifting that goes on in the inner chambers of a marriage. We see the nakedness, the scramble to cover.

This is the moment of our rebellion, the provocation of the curse. If you'd asked me when I was growing up to describe the curse, I'd tell you it was the proclamation that we go to hell if we don't ask Jesus into our hearts. There are certainly eternal implications to the events of the story in Genesis. But what strikes me now about the curse of chapter 3 is what is *actually* stated. The wording reads a bit differently than our assigned meaning and internalized analysis of it.

Here, in the immediate aftermath of this colossally consequential mistake, in this turning point of history and pronouncement of our fate, nothing of hell or asking Jesus to come into our hearts is mentioned. Instead, God starts talking about snakes, and babies, and thorns and thistles. God starts talking about work. It's an odd edict for our twenty-first-century ears. Certainly, the consequences of sin, bodily death, and our need for a Savior will follow in the story and texts to come. But what could possibly be going on here, precisely in the proclamation of Genesis 3, and how will it impact the future of the world?

Our origin story is one of both blessing and curse. Scholars tell us the word for "curse" in Hebrew should be understood to mean the opposite of "blessing." If blessing is the presence of God's favor, then a curse is the removal of God's favor. Its closest equivalent is the word "damn."[14] The deceiving snake is the first to receive an imprecation, a future of crawling shamefully on his belly and eating the dust, despised and crushed by humankind. God goes on to describe the curse of the pain of childbearing for the woman, the brokenness that will exist between the woman and the man, and finally the curse of the ground in Genesis 3:17–19:

Cursed is the ground because of you;
through painful toil you will eat food from it
all the days of your life.
It will produce thorns and thistles for you,
and you will eat the plants of the field.
By the sweat of your brow
you will eat your food.

When the ground was blessed, it produced equal return for our investment. Work brought joy and fulfillment. Now that the ground is cursed, fruit bearing, as with the anguish of childbearing, requires a painful toil. The ground is unable to cooperate with us fully. The original meaning and purpose of work is distorted and perverted; it becomes a chore, a grind, and a slog.[15]

Pastor and theologian Tim Keller asks the question, "What do we mean when we say work is fruitless? We mean that, in all our work, we will be able to envision far more than we can accomplish, both because of a lack of ability and because of resistance in the environment around us."[16] We sow seeds, but we reap thorns and thistles. The fruit from the garden is replaced by briar and bramble, worthless and demoralizing. The barrenness of the ground leads to a barrenness of being.

Fundamental to our understanding of what it means to be human and to be broken is to understand that the beautiful, fulfilling, rewarding work to which we were called is no longer consistently beautiful, fulfilling, and rewarding. The holy undertaking of labor has been marred, and we are constantly seeking to replace that holiness with our own fraudulent forms of piety and self-importance. The priestly duties have been squandered.

Theologian David Fagerberg put it this way: "The fall is the forfeiture of our liturgical career."[17]

Ceɔ

The implications of the curse of the ground are all around us, in big and small ways. Sometimes the effect is catastrophic. Other times, it is simply inconvenient. Just before sitting down to write this, I spent a good half hour folding laundry, only to have my toddler come barreling through the living room, tossing my neat piles into the air with glee.

Once, my sister, a highly acclaimed author, spilled an entire mug of chai tea on her laptop. It saturated the hard drive and she lost about one fourth of the manuscript she'd been working on for months. Hours and hours of thought, research, wordsmithing, and artistry were lost.

I have a friend from high school who purchased an old, run-down house in my hometown when she was first married. Room by room, she and her husband renovated that home, gutting and remaking the kitchen and bathrooms, reflooring and painting, finishing stairs, and adding spaces for sleeping as each of their four children was born. Last week, the entire home was destroyed in a fire. No one in the family was hurt, but a decade's worth of slow, meticulous labor was gone. Memories, family treasures, and a labor of love burned to ashes.

I know aid workers who serve in countries many would consider failed states. They spend years writing proposals for funding, planning for programming, investing in communities, and building relationships only to have all their work shut down because of political violence and warfare. Warehouses of food are ransacked, schools are looted, and boreholes where women once fetched clean water are destroyed.

Gardens get eaten by pests. Weeds grow up among the fruit. Poverty rears its ugly head, and injustice strikes again. Spreadsheets are lost. Boredom sets in. Koi fish die in the mud. We sow seeds, yet we reap thorns and thistles.

Find the job you love, and you'll never work a day in your life?

Hard labor is an essential reality of being human. The emotional prosperity gospel minimizes the curse, forgets the fact that our environment is hostile toward our efforts. *Work is not cursed.* But the ground of our labor is inhospitable to bounty, to satisfaction, to fulfillment. When you experience the disappointment of frustrated labor, you are experiencing the heart of the curse, an edict that is ancient and adept. Our souls recognize it even when we choose not to name it. It is no anomaly to be disappointed by work, no indication of failure or miscalculation on your part. You will never find the perfect job that nullifies this curse. In truth, there is nothing more human than to experience frustrated labor. We join with our brothers and sisters, with our ancestors, and with future generations when we cry out to God in our pain. To lament the difficulty of work is to sing a chorus as old as time itself. Maybe it sounds strange, but I find that to be deeply comforting.

If it is the ground that is cursed, rather than work itself, I have to believe that there is still dignity and even joy to be found in our labor if we pay attention. I've traveled to enough economically disadvantaged regions of the world to know that work, and the provision it can bring, is a gift. I think this is why Tim is so committed to our little garden. He has a knack for noticing the fruit hidden among the thorns, of seeing things as they were meant to be. Whether farmer, fisherman, pastor, or CEO, when we work, we imitate our Creator. Work is not a mechanism by which we earn value and prove our worth. When we labor, we demonstrate the dignity that is already ours simply by virtue of being the image bearers of a divine laborer. To work is to be human in the Garden of Eden. To be frustrated by work is to be human in the aftermath of the fall.

In working, Adam and Eve basked in the likeness of their Creator and reveled in the wonder of the presence of God. Likewise, in working we display our humanity. We boast in God, our Creator and sustainer. When we grieve the difficulty of work, we actually worship. *We say, This is not the garden our good God designed.*

I can't help but marvel at the poetic nature of God. On the cross, at the moment of our redemption, when death itself was put to death and the curse of the fall was stripped of its power, Christ wore not a crown of gold or silver, but a crown of thorns, the emblem of our frustration. It was as if he was thumbing his nose at the curse. And I wonder sometimes if we could do the same. Maybe our most powerful act of resistance to the curse is to plant a garden. To save some koi fish. When we persevere, through the spreadsheets and the meetings, the droughts and the pests, the boredom and the failure, the harvest and the bounty, the injustices and the rewards, the thorns and the thistles, we harken back to our priestly vocation in the Garden of Eden. Our frustration is a reminder that we were made for the perfect presence of God. When we work, we long for his presence, and that is a worthy endeavor in and of itself.

CHAPTER 2

MARRIAGE

(Marry the Love of Your Life)

Five years after my wedding, I found myself sitting alone on a couch in the office of our marriage counselor. The room was chilly from the air conditioner, and I was covered in goosebumps. Pastel landscape paintings lined the walls and a little stuffed Winnie the Pooh toy sat on a bookshelf next to psychology textbooks and various publications on family systems theories and childhood trauma.

Pooh and the counselor stared at me, waiting for me to speak. I'd sought a private session with the counselor, dissatisfied with the progress we were making in the sessions where Tim was present. I thought I'd catch the counselor alone, give her the real scoop on what was happening between Tim and me, win her to my side, make her my ally.

I began to dish, telling her all of Tim's shortcomings, outlining with my very impressive vocabulary the various transgressions and offenses. I made my case, allowed the tears to trickle pitifully from my eyes. She nodded and blinked at me. Pooh grimaced. I waited for her impassioned affirmation of my righteous indignation at Tim.

"I see," she said.

Ha! *She sees!*

"Well, Amanda, it seems like the solution here is for you to maybe…find some good girl friends? You know, develop relationships with other people who can help meet some of your relational and emotional needs."

My face flushed. She couldn't be serious. "Oh, I *have friends*," I retorted back. I looked to Pooh, who now seemed strangely ambivalent. The counselor smiled coolly back at me as if to say, "I bet you do."

I broke out in a sweat despite the chill. In that moment, it sounded like she was giving up on Tim, abandoning any hope that my marriage could be happy. I was furious. I was paying her to fix my marriage, to fix Tim! What kind of solution was this? Make more friends? What good could friends possibly do when your relationship with the person who was supposed to be the love of your life was on the rocks?

I left her office in a huff and never went back. Breaking up with your marriage counselor when you are tempted to break up with your husband was a new low.

Scholars have struggled to determine the exact function and meaning of marriage throughout history. It is difficult to state with certainty how and why the practice of male and female unions first emerged in the prehistoric era. Was it primarily a way to organize the division of labor between men and women? Was it a system for regulating sexuality or "legitimizing" children? Did it serve as a mechanism for the redistribution of resources to dependents? Or was it all of the above?[1]

Whatever the case may be, throughout most of history, love or romance was rarely ever the primary reason a man and woman wed. Marriages have typically been arranged by parents or guardians. Social, political, and financial advantages were the main considerations, not the affection that existed—or did not exist— between the couple. For royal, aristocratic, and upper-class society, a favorable marriage was a way of gaining influence, consolidating power, and acquiring wealth. For peasants and the working class, a strategic match was a way of building a secure workforce within the home and community. Marriage was not the business of two people. It was the business of an entire web of social affiliations.

It's not that people from the past did not enjoy a good love story. Passion and romance weave their way through ancient dramas, mythology, ballads, and folktales. Historian Stephanie Coontz writes, "People have always loved a love story. But for most of the past our ancestors did not try to live in one."[2]

In fact, couples were often warned against the dangers of love in marriage. Affection between husbands and wives was seen as a potential threat to the social order provided by the union. In ancient China, for example, it was believed that if a husband had too much fondness for his wife, he might choose her interests over the interests of his parents, who expected to maintain control over his time and labor. In ancient India, falling in love before marriage was seen as deeply disruptive. Agrarian and plebeian cultures throughout the ages have often scoffed at marital intimacy because an affectionate husband and wife might retreat inward and neglect the wider web of social support.[3]

So what happened? How did romantic love become the catalyst for marriage and the most revered form of love in society?

It was a slow process. Some trace the change back to the Protestant Reformation. Contesting the Catholic Church's exaltation of the priesthood and celibacy, Martin Luther declared that Christians in all stations of life and in every vocation could honor God as effectively as any minister or monastic. He and other Reformers began writing and preaching about the value of marriage, describing it not as an inferior calling but rather as God's best for both men and women.[4]

The Catholic Church, of course, pushed back. "If anyone says that the married state excels the state of virginity or celibacy, and that it is better and happier to be united in matrimony than to remain in virginity or celibacy, let him be anathema," declared the Council of Trent in 1563.[5]

But the Council could not stop the tide of history. Times were changing and there were other forces at work in favor of love. The growth of wage labor meant that young people were less dependent on the economic life force of the extended family structure. People could leave the farm, as it were, and venture out on their own. Individuals increasingly had the freedom and ability to make their own choice of marriage partner based on tastes and personal preference.

Popular novels of the eighteenth and nineteenth centuries began exploring the domestic lives of ordinary people and the sweetness of love shared between husband and wife.[6] Leaders of the Enlightenment preached the value of "the pursuit of happiness."

Why not seek happiness within marriage? These slow but steady changes in society eventually "shifted the basis of marriage from sharing tasks to sharing feelings," writes Coontz. "The older view that wives and husbands were work mates gave way to [the] idea that they were soul mates."[7]

Husbands and wives—particularly those in the middle and upper classes—continued to grow in independence from the network of neighbors and extended family. New couples would often move to a new community or new city, far away from relatives, and start fresh. The nuclear family—husband, wife, and children in a single household—gradually became the building block of society.[8]

As love, rather than politics and economics, became the basis for marriage, the tide of public opinion began to turn regarding divorce. If falling in love was a good enough reason to marry, then falling out of love was a good enough reason to divorce. Many people started thinking it was immoral to remain in a loveless marriage. Throughout the 1800s, divorce laws began to loosen, and by the mid-1900s most Western countries had passed laws that allowed divorce due simply to irreconcilable differences.[9]

These days many of our expectations surrounding marriage are derived less from the Bible and more from *Leave It to Beaver*. The postwar era of the 1950s and '60s was considered the golden age of marriage. The instability of the Great Depression and World War II likely drove people toward the stability of marriage. People were marrying at young ages and—with rising life expectancy—were staying married longer. Writes Coontz:

> In this unique period in Western history, marriage pro-
> vided the context for just about every piece of most people's

lives. Marriage was how practically everyone embarked on his or her "real" life. It was the institution that moved you through life's stages. And it was where you expected to be when your life ended.[10]

Singleness became an increasingly marginalized status. In a 1957 survey in the United States, four out of five respondents indicated that they believed people who preferred to remain single were "sick," "neurotic," or "immoral."[11] Participation in monasteries and convents, which traditionally were establishments where celibates could experience lifelong communal commitment, has continued to decline, with the number of nuns in the United States dropping by 72.5 percent since the mid-1960s.[12] Today, as the definition of traditional marriage has been challenged and people increasingly opt to cohabitate before tying the knot, many people still believe that a romantic partner is the most important relationship in life.

These days, we still love a good love story, but we fancy ourselves the main characters. Our radical individualism has converged with our romantic idealism. Finding the love of your life is the linchpin of a happy life. Romantic partnership is the ultimate form of self-expression and self-actualization—the way we feel most seen and validated in this world. We build every expectation of a blessed future on the foundation of a contented nuclear family. Our spouse is our confidant, kindred spirit, lover, and soulmate. They are our happily ever after.

Many centuries ago, in what is now Jiangyong's Shungjian Xu Township, a fertile valley in the southwestern corner of Hunan Province in China, a language spoken and written only by women emerged. In a culture dictated by tradition and social hierarchies, women of that era and region were not permitted to learn to read and write Chinese. So, they came up with their own form of communication. Scholars believe that *nushu*, a single-sex language and perhaps the only one of its kind in the world, was born within the ancient custom of "sworn sisters," a tight sorority of village girls who pledged lifelong loyalty and friendship with one another. These girls would grow up together, learning to keep house, to weave and embroider...and to speak and write nushu.

This close-knit sisterhood was inevitably shattered by marriage, whereby a bride was expected to go away to her groom's home. To depart from those beautiful bonds of friendship, from the shared learning and labor, and to enter an unfamiliar family with new expectations and responsibilities was frightening and grievous. It was during this transition that the language of nushu played its most important role.

Three days after her wedding, the young bride would receive from her sworn sisters a "Third Day Book," a cloth-bound volume that was a diary of sorts. The first few pages would already be filled with nushu script, notes and messages from her sisters and her mother lamenting the loss of their friend and daughter. They were expressions of deep sorrow at the change that marriage had brought about and also expressions of hope for happiness in her future as a wife. Because the messages were written in nushu, the groom could not read the sentiments. In the blank pages that remained, the new bride would record her own laments, hopes,

and reflections on her new life. The book would become a trea-
sured, lifelong journal—a place where a woman could express her
own thoughts and feelings in a mysterious and intimate script
known only to other women.[13]

The thought that marriage could be a grievous transition was
foreign to me. No one ever told me that I should lament the end of
my singleness, that to gain a husband was to also lose many things
I held dear: autonomy, independence, total freedom of choice.

I was only ever told that marriage was the preferred option. The
words of Paul were conveniently ignored: "Now to the unmarried
and the widows I say: It is good for them to stay unmarried…I wish
that all of you were as I am [single]" (1 Cor. 7:8, 7). I was taught
that marriage was God's design, that being a wife and mother was
the highest calling to which a woman could aspire. The message
was subtle but clear: "Spinsters" or "bachelors" were to be pitied,
and marriage was to be esteemed.

"You complete me,"an ardent Jerry Maguire says to Dorothy
in an iconic moment of Hollywood romance. Somehow, I took the
Old Testament idea that "it is not good for the man to be alone"
(Gen. 2:18) to mean "it is not good for *me* to be without a *man*
who loves me and needs me desperately." I knew marriage would
have its ups and downs, but I imagined that the fights would end
with a warm embrace, the character flaws would be dissolved by
our mutual sanctification, and the differences of opinion would
somehow merge together as we journeyed through our bright and
beautiful future together.

I never imagined that I'd miss being single so much, that I'd
long for the days when I could go out or spend money or make a
decision without running it by someone else. I never anticipated

the nights filled with the hollow fear of wondering if I'd made the worst mistake of my life in marrying Tim. I never expected the man I loved most in the world to feel like a stranger. It was a loneliness like I'd never experienced before, and I had no language like nushu to express it. I *had* no permission to feel the way I was feeling. I never knew I was capable of such anger, such profound rage at someone for not being perfect. For not making me happy.

Throughout the ages, marriage has often been considered the antidote for maladies, both social and physical, that have plagued women. Ancient Greco-Roman physicians identified a condition known as the "wandering womb." They believed that if the *hysterika* (the uterus) remained inactive or ungratified for too long, it would begin migrating around the body in search of fluid. This migration would cause abnormal behavior, or hysteria, in women. Writes neurologist J. M. S. Pearce, "Certain Hippocratic texts give graphic descriptions of the uterus as a restless animal, furiously raging through the female...which produced bizarre symptoms including a sensation of suffocation, palpitations, and aphonia [the inability to speak]."[14] The most obvious solution to these symptoms, naturally, was marital sex and pregnancy, which was thought to relocate the womb to its proper anatomical location.

I don't recall a pastor ever telling me that my uterus was wandering. But I do remember being told that marriage and, consequently, motherhood would make me a better person, that it was the purpose for which I was created. Biblical womanhood was best embodied in the roles of wife and mom. I was told that within marriage I would experience the sanctification God most desired. Through submission and self-sacrifice I would know what it meant to truly surrender to God.

In centuries past, Protestant, Catholic, and Muslim teachers alike warned that excessive romantic love within marriage could lead to idolatry or diminishing love for God. But growing up, I remember pastors telling me about the importance of a husband "dating" his wife to keep the passion alive. They would brag from the pulpit about their "smokin' hot" wives and the abiding affection they shared for one another. I saw triangular charts indicating that as I grew closer to my husband, I'd grow closer to God.

"Marriage is seen as a form of spiritual credentialing," says author and journalist Katelyn Beaty.[15] This elevation of marriage as the sure path to holiness is reflected in the operational designs of our faith communities. Resources and programming are often geared toward supporting couples and nuclear families rather than single people. Women in particular who are unmarried or are career-minded testify that they struggle to find validation in the church context.[16]

Beaty observes that the evangelical church's teaching on sexuality and purity has created many false expectations for young people. Christian teenagers growing up in the '90s like me were inundated with the True Love Waits movement, which urged kids to remain sexually pure until their wedding night. This movement, Beaty posits, "holds that God will reward premarital chastity with a good Christian spouse, great sex, and perpetual marital fulfillment." Beaty calls this "the sexual prosperity gospel."

She writes: "Sexual prosperity theology was supposed to

combat the mainstream culture's embrace of no-strings-attached sex and sex education in public schools." Proponents of this teaching "held out the ultimate one-up to secular licentiousness: God wants to give you a hot spouse and great sex life, as long as you wait."[17]

With all these expectations making their way into the bloodstream of American evangelical youths, it is understandable why singles end up feeling like second-class citizens. It makes sense that when met with the trials and disappointments of a *real* marriage, many couples want to give up. When marriage fails to consistently deliver on the promise of holistic happiness—spiritual sanctification, sexual gratification, and relational fulfillment—a Christian couple can feel like they are anomalous, irreparably broken. It is no wonder that Christian marriages end at roughly the same rate as non-Christian marriages.[18]

Unfortunately, Christians rarely speak openly and honestly about the difficulties experienced in marriage. Yes, we may refer vaguely to the challenges, may mention the quibbles or moments of disagreement. But few people speak with specificity and vulnerability about how heartbreaking a relationship with your spouse can be.

"A good marriage requires work and dedication," the older women gently told me at my bridal showers, smiling reminiscently. "Give and take," they said, patting my arm, "grace and understanding." They looked more nostalgic than battle-weary, so I filed away the word of advice with little thought or concern.

They didn't tell me I'd be white-knuckling my way to my one-year anniversary. They didn't tell me just how many nights the sun would go down on my anger and then rise again in the morning on my weary resentment. They didn't tell me how necessary marriage counseling would be, how desperate I'd become for intervention, how ashamed I'd feel for being unhappy. In my mind, only truly broken people with really messed-up relationships went to marriage counseling. Every married person I knew *seemed* happy. So I just assumed that hard, I mean really and truly *difficult*, was abnormal. Unhappy was abnormal.

Tim and I started arguing when we were engaged. I don't remember exactly what the spats were about, but I do remember wondering if it was wise and responsible for us to go through with the marriage. I considered ending the engagement, but I've always been terribly concerned about what people think about me, and I didn't want to embarrass myself or Tim.

Also, I loved him, so there was that.

I remember falling into bed the night before our wedding thinking I must be the only woman in the history of the world who wasn't blissfully happy to be walking down the aisle. I was filled with doubt, with questions, with uncertainty. But I was also clinging to the hope that once we actually said our vows and sealed the deal, God would kick that marital sanctification into gear, and we'd be fine. Of course, anyone who has been married knows that saying "I do" is no silver bullet.

As the years passed and the challenges continued, I thought Tim had failed, or I had failed, or God had failed. This thing that was supposed to be making me a better person seemed to be having the opposite effect. So, I devoured marriage books, but few of them helped. I was told that I needed love and that Tim needed respect. I learned about each of our preferred love languages. I tried to set healthy boundaries. Still, my marriage seemed to be floundering. I'd fly into fits of rage and poor Tim, eager to help but unsure what to say, would eventually just shrug his shoulders and ask if I wanted to watch TV. My rage increased.

You might even say I was hysterical.

Here's the thing. Deep down I knew my expectations for marriage must be pretty high because Tim—though certainly imperfect like every other human who's ever lived—is actually a pretty awesome person. Ask anyone who knows him: He's selfless, low drama, hardworking, smart, sacrificial, funny, gentle, and caring. He is super agreeable, and he has never made me feel unsafe. If I wasn't happy in my marriage, I suspected no one could be.

Looking back, it's safe to say that the root of most of our marital disputes has been more about differing temperaments than overt sin. Our families had each managed conflict very differently. The cultural gap between Midwesterners and Southerners is *vast*.

When we were engaged and newly married, we did what any good young Christian couple should do when there is conflict: We went to our pastor. He pulled out the Bible and directed us to all the go-to marriage passages. He asked us to each examine our hearts and repent of whatever sin it was that was leading us to argue. He told me to submit, and he told Tim to lead. He gave us verses to read and prayers to pray with one another.

Being encouraged to read the Bible is never a bad thing. The Scriptures have always defined for me what it meant to treat someone with dignity. They teach me what love looks like and that every person, even my spouse, is worthy of being treated as an image bearer of God.

But another subtle lie of the emotional prosperity gospel had crept into my marriage. The belief was that if you just read your Bible, do what it says, and stop sinning, all your relational challenges will magically disappear. Our pastor never talked to us about family systems or personality differences. He never investigated the source of our conflict or how past hurts might be impeding us. He never normalized the tension or told us that maybe our disagreements were merely part of the process of learning about one another, adjusting to the labor of sharing life together. Instead, he gave us a very simple and precise formula.

Obey God and your marriage will be happy. Follow the traditional roles of husband and wife, and things will improve. Repent, and all will be well.

It's taken me almost a decade to realize it, but the best marriage advice I've ever been given by far was from that awful, wonderful counselor who told me to "go get some friends." *And*, incidentally, from Winnie the Pooh: "A day without a friend is like a pot without a single drop of honey left inside."[19]

My counselor was right. I needed more friends, needed to expand my relational support. She was not giving up on my marriage. Rather, she had identified in me an expectation that had set my marriage up for failure. No one person can possibly meet all our practical, emotional, and spiritual needs. No one person holds the keys to our happily ever after. It takes a village, not just to raise a child, but to survive as a human. We need each other. We need friends, coworkers, mentors, ministers, parents, siblings, and neighbors to journey with us through this perilous world.

C. S. Lewis wrote, "To the Ancients, Friendship seemed the

happiest and most fully human of all loves; the crown of life and the school of virtue. The modern world, in comparison, ignores it."[20] He laments the fact that our tributes to the glory of friendship in the arts and literature are so few and far between. We have very few modern equivalents of Jonathan and David, Roland and Oliver, Hamlet and Horatio.

Instead, we are fed a steady diet of romantic love stories from the day we emerge from the womb: damsels in distress being rescued by the charming prince, love songs on the radio, the rom-com genre that dominated the silver screen in the 1990s and 2000s, reality dating shows. What we see in our media, we expect to experience ourselves. Life feels incomplete without a romantic partner because we are so often told that it is.

"You deserve a fairy-tale ending." It's something I've heard said in the movies, on TV, in song, and in my dorm room at my Christian college. "You deserve *your* happily ever after," and by "happily ever after," we mean a romantic partner who will make us the center of their world. Somewhere out there, the love of your life is waiting for you, ready to make all your dreams come true.

While the world was becoming obsessed with romance and marriage, it was losing its appreciation for other forms of love and commitment. Convents and monasteries aren't the only communal institutions that are in decline. Membership in groups, from bowling clubs and rotary clubs to Boy Scouts and Girl Scouts, is waning in popularity.[21] With the rise of suburban, nuclear family–centered households comes an overall decrease in intergenerational households, particularly for middle-class white families.[22] The days of co-laboring in the fields, of "calling" on your neighbors without invitation, of visiting with one another on front porches seem like a distant memory.

This means that the spouse alone is expected to carry the huge load of our interpersonal and social needs. We expect them to be friend, adviser, lover, playmate, cheerleader, co-parent, economic partner, and confidant. We even expect husbands to pastor wives. Many Christians told me that Tim was supposed to be my spiritual leader. As the head of our marriage, he was to serve as the intermediary between me and God. No wonder our marriage began to buckle. No man, or woman for that matter, could possibly bear the weight of all that pressure.

God as husband, the Church as his bride—this analogy should never supersede the wide and beautiful array of familial images Scripture presents to us. God is like a mother (see Isa. 66:13). God is like a father (see Matt. 6:9). We are his children (see John 1:12). Jesus is our brother (see Heb. 2:11). He is our friend (see John 15:14).

And we (the Church) are siblings. When Paul tells believers to love one another as brothers and sisters, he is asking them to enter into a relational commitment that, in the ancient world, was every bit as important as marriage.[23] It is only as a family of God that we can experience the fullness of life together, with all its diversity of affections. The idolization of romantic love harms married people because it creates false expectations. Likewise, the idolization of romantic love harms single people because it insinuates a lack of wholeness. When a perfect marriage is implied to be the primary path to happiness and righteousness, the attainment of it can become all-consuming.

Redistributing the load of my emotional needs to people other than Tim—like friends, mentors, colleagues, and pastors—acted as a relief valve in my marriage. Once our relationship was released from the pressure to be perfect, it was suddenly free to just *be*. No, it wasn't flawless. But it was actually really, really good. I began to savor my life with Tim for all that it was instead of resenting it for all that it was not.

And I began to savor other relationships too. I began to share more intimately with my friends. I went to mentors for advice. I learned to depend on neighbors and co-workers. I expanded beyond the walls of my house. I built a home within my community, not just under the roof with my husband. As strange as it sounds, once I began expecting less of my marriage, it was finally able to be more. And once I began expecting more of my other relationships, the load of life became amazingly lighter.

Being tethered to Tim has indeed been a grace in my life. Our union has met many of the marital objectives valued throughout history. Our marriage was financially advantageous (my husband is gainfully employed). It divided the labors of homemaking (I cook; he cleans up). It ensured our meager resources would be passed down a clear line of inheritors (we have two children together). And I suppose it even solidified a few new social alliances (Tim was successfully converted into an Alabama football fan and now I always root for the Green Bay Packers).

But the privilege Tim and I have always enjoyed as a couple is that we chose each other. We met through mutual friends at a Christmas party and fell in love rather quickly. The first time we spoke on the phone, we talked until his cell battery died. It all felt very romantic.

And I am grateful to say that on many days, it still does.

But then, of course, there are the days when it does not. We live in a world where we are told that love—whether in marriage or in friendship—is only as good as our emotional experience of it. If the relationship doesn't bring emotional fulfillment, it must be bad. If a friendship doesn't always buoy the ego, it must be a failure. If my husband doesn't bring about all my hopes and dreams, then he must be wrong for me.

But emotional pain is always a risk of proximity, whether that proximity exists in marriage, friendship, discipleship, or teamwork. Over the years, Tim and I have grown closer to each other. Closer to one another's virtues. Closer to one another's vices. Closer to one another's strengths and weaknesses. Closer to one another's humanity. The fact that I argue with Tim more than anyone else in my life is a testament not to flaws in our character (though those abound) but rather to the amount of time we spend with each other. We share most meals, spend every weekend together, sleep in the same bed. Disagreements are bound to arise. It's just the mathematics of immediacy, the hazards of nearness.

Truth be told, much of my frustration at my spouse is not so much disappointment with him as much as it is frustration with life. Because we do so much of life together, I identify Tim with all the hard, tiring, and paltry demands existence places on us. When the dishwasher breaks, I call Tim. When the toilet clogs, I call Tim. When an unexpected bill breaks our budget, I call Tim. We've seen each other sick with stomach bugs and cleaned up one another's vomit. And there are deeper emotional wounds that I associate with Tim. We've joined and left churches together. We've experienced three miscarriages together. We've grieved the loss of siblings and grandparents and friends together. When life gets hard, Tim is not my enemy. But he is the easiest target. Guilty by association.

There is certainly a difference between difficult and dangerous. There are some relationships that are truly unsafe, both emotionally and physically. Abuse is never something that should be normalized or simply endured. It must be named, escaped, condemned, and prosecuted when necessary. My marriage was never dangerous or damaging. It was just uncomfortable. Deeply so at times. It was uncomfortable because sticking with my commitment required me to resist every urge instilled in me by my secular culture. It even required me to think beyond some of the expectations and strict paradigms that had been given to me by the Church.

In the poem "Adam's Curse," W. B. Yeats writes:

It's certain there is no fine thing
Since Adam's fall but needs much labouring.[24]

Beauty. Art. Work. Love. All good, true, and noble things require effort. And that effort has been marred by the curse. "Your desire will be for your husband, and he will rule over you" (Gen. 3:16). While scholars have litigated the exact meaning of this difficult text for centuries, suffice it to say the purity of the relationship between men and women has been tarnished by selfishness, power, and strife that play out in myriad ways in various cultures and time periods. Yeats goes on:

I had a thought for no one's but your ears:
That you were beautiful, and that I strove
To love you in the old high way of love;
That it had all seemed happy, and yet we'd grown
As weary-hearted as that hollow moon.[25]

Love can indeed enhance your happiness. And sometimes, it can make you weary-hearted. Frustrated. To think of love as a labor has been helpful to me as I've processed the ups and downs of my marriage. Just like the ground of our labor is cursed, the soil in which relationships bud, bloom, and grow is very often inhospitable to our flourishing. Gardening requires a gentle kind of patience and persistence. So does marriage or any intimate relationship. Our ancestors' view of love—that old "high way"—saw matrimony less as a fairy tale and more as a yoking, a binding together of co-workers in the field of life. Happiness is not what makes a marriage holy. What makes it so sacred is not its emotional euphoria but rather its permanence. What makes marriage unique is that it is a lifelong oath.

Life is indeed long, and sometimes disheartening. Yes, there is guilt by association. But there is also camaraderie by association. Deep respect. Profound gratefulness. Tim and I have done hard things, but we have done them together. Life has required us to be so much more than romantic partners. We've both committed to the labor of our love, to the labor of our shared lives.

Not every marriage produces children. That does not mean that marriage is broken. Not every marriage meets our romantic expectations. That does not mean it is broken. Not every marriage is an equally shared yoke in every season. That does not mean it is broken. Not every marriage is the picture of happiness at all times. That does not mean it is broken. And not all people choose to or have the opportunity to get married. That does not make them broken. Romantic love is not the highest form of love, and marital "bliss" is not the highest form of happiness. Marriage is indeed a crucible of sanctification. But so is any relationship in which vulnerability, duty, and sacrifice are present. There are many stations in life that forge our souls, and none can be ranked as holier than another. Love, commitment, and proximity in *all* their forms make us better, make life more beautiful, and mend the brokenness.

I've come to believe that there is an ancient beauty in the binding of oneself to another—whether as spouses, colleagues, co-ministers, mentors, mentees, church members, or neighbors. We can accomplish so much more together. It feels true to our creation mandate to care for one another and to care for the world *together*. It is right and wondrous to bear witness to each other in proximate ways—in vulnerable ways. Indeed, no one person can carry the burden of all our emotional and relational needs. But when we stand shoulder to shoulder as a community of faith, we can carry an astounding load.

I have often struggled with marriage as an institution, balked at the work it required, chafed when my pride was wounded or my hopes disappointed. Marriage is not a shortcut to "the good life." It is not a fairy tale or the be-all and end-all. But the promise itself is a beautiful safeguard that ensures I stay true to what I know is right and good in the long run. It is a type of insurance against my own tendency to fight or flee whenever things get tough. In a world where vows seem like they were made to be broken, there is something subversive about giving more power to your promise than to your preference, about giving more credence to your commitment than to impulse. And a promise, when carefully tended, can become a wonderfully powerful form of love.

CHAPTER 3

PARENTHOOD

(Have Lots of Kids)

Eve. It was the name given to the first woman who ever breathed the air of this good earth. The Hebrew word *chavvah*, meaning "life" or "giver or preserver of the living," was appointed to her, for she was destined to be the mother of humankind, to give birth to the generations.

The verse in Genesis chapter 3 that names Eve—verse 20—feels abrupt in the text, a bit out of place. The curse—the punishment for the sin of eating the forbidden fruit—is pronounced in verses 14 through 19. The aftermath of the curse—the expulsion from the garden—is described in verses 21 through 24. But in the middle, we see Adam naming Eve as the mother of a great lineage to come. It is a quiet injection of hope, the whispered recognition that despite their disobedience, something surprising has happened. They will be permitted to go on living. New life will come, generations will follow, and the earth will still maintain some sense of goodness.[1]

"Be fruitful and multiply," the man and woman are told in the garden. In fact, this is the first command given to humans by God according to the Genesis chapter 1 account. Many millennia later, I feel the reverberations of this ancient mandate shuddering deep within my own anatomy. I am a daughter of Eve. My very frame tells me there is a sacred task that is mine.

"God has made her body to be with man, to bear children and to raise them," Martin Luther wrote in 1524, "as is evident by the members of the body ordered by God Himself."[2] Almost five hundred years later, Reverend Walter J. Chantry preached, "Woman's hope, the church's hope, the world's hope is joined to childbearing with continuance in faith, love and holiness. Young women, here is a life-long calling! It is the highest any woman can enter."[3]

This veneration of the woman's womb all sounded very inspiring to me until, at age thirty-three, I found myself sitting on the bathroom floor with yet another negative pregnancy test in hand and hope, once again, seeping from my body. Month after month, year after year, I had slowly discovered that *my* body, actually, was not made to create life. At least not easily.

The notion that a woman's greatest calling was to bear children has been around since long before the days of Martin Luther, but the concept has experienced a strong revival in the Church in the wake of the feminist movement of the 1950s and '60s. The emerging secular culture was telling women that they should shake off the shackles of motherhood and housekeeping and pursue their *real* potential by climbing the corporate ladder and chasing their professional dreams. In response, faith leaders set out to convince women that there was, in fact, dignity in diaper changing. We were to glory in our role as reproducers. To serve as a mother was to be faithful to God's unique design. It was the highest feminine aspiration, the surest path to true happiness.

It is through service in the home that a woman makes her greatest impact in the kingdom.

None of these preachers prepared me for infertility. It was a pain that wasn't talked about, grief that was hidden from view. In an effort to cajole my womb into cooperation, I went to specialists, took a cocktail of obscure supplements, ate raw and organic foods, scoured the internet for antidotes, read all the books, and learned all the folk remedies. I prayed the prayers of the barren biblical matriarchs: Sarah, Rebekah, Rachel, and Hannah. I was determined that by sheer force of will, I could make new life happen for *me*.

When I did finally get pregnant, I certainly wasn't counting on the baby not to survive past the ninth week of pregnancy. A standard ten-week ultrasound revealed that the little heart that I'd seen steadily pumping three weeks earlier had now stopped, forever still. I'd not felt any different, had not detected a change. I wasn't bleeding, wasn't cramping. How could my entire future with this tiny, perfect miracle have collapsed without me even noticing? Where was my maternal intuition when I most needed it? "Are you sure?" I kept saying to the doctor, "Absolutely sure?" She was crying and nodding, thrusting a box of tissues in my face. She was sure. As for me, I had no tears—just an empty disbelief that this could possibly be part of God's plan.

The idea that my womb was inhospitable to life, averse to my God-given purpose as a woman, was crushing. What would I do, and who would I be if I could not have a baby? For a long time, my status as a mother stalled out in the "expecting" stage. Those expectations—of blessing and of purpose—were exceedingly high and only grew as the years went by with them unmet. To feel betrayed by my own body has been, to this day, the most anxiety-inducing experience of my life. I couldn't understand what I had done wrong. It was as if I was simultaneously culpable and powerless, filled with both hope and despair. I've never known self-reproach like that before, never known a more gnawing unhappiness. I just wanted it to be over, just wanted to hold the future I desired in my arms.

The infertile woman knows better than most that all life is truly a miracle, that no amount of coercion can force a baby into existence. God gives life, but he does not give it to all. Sometimes he takes it away. I carried that knowledge around like an ever-present ache in my belly. So, when I eventually did become pregnant with a baby that grew as expected, kicked my ribs, and plundered my body of every ounce of energy, I was filled with bliss. And bewilderment.

I'd always heard pregnancy was the most natural experience a woman can ever know. But so far, nothing about the undertaking felt natural to me. There is nothing natural about hormone-induced cycles and stuffing prescribed meds down your throat in an effort to stay pregnant. There's nothing natural about craving potato chips for breakfast. There's nothing natural about watching your hands and feet swell to the size of sausages. There's nothing normal about waddling into the hospital, spreading your legs in a room full of strangers, pushing a wriggling, wailing human being out of your own body, and then going home the next day with the expectation that you will keep that human alive and love it forever.

I rode home in our Honda with that little baby—still wriggling—in the back seat and Tim driving twenty miles under the speed limit. I had the wide-eyed feeling of having just experienced a beautiful and breathtaking trauma. In the span of just a few years, I had longed for a baby, lost a baby, and then birthed a baby. I'd grown an actual human in my body and somehow released it into the world. She'd gone from the size of a poppy seed to the size of a small pumpkin, had pressed in and displaced all my insides until she—and I—needed to be delivered. She was exposed to the world now, to the elements, to the pain and potential cruelty of existence. It was my job to make sure she didn't starve, didn't freeze, didn't get taken. My life was no longer my own. I had outgrown all my most trusted coping mechanisms.

Somehow, I knew even then that my body would never be the same, that the miracle I'd prayed for had come with a cost. It was more than the labor and delivery. My brain chemistry felt altered. The emotional landscape of my life was forever changed. I was covered in stretch marks, from my belly to my heart to my head.

Wonder has its place, but it is not the only skill you need as a parent. It didn't take me long to realize that parenting itself did not come instinctually to me. I didn't have much experience with kids—had never been a babysitter or worked in the church nursery. To me newborns looked and acted like aliens—wrinkled, squirmy, and squealing. I didn't know how to hold them or what to say to them. I didn't know what was normal. I was convinced my own baby was going to just stop breathing at some point and that it would be all my fault.

My husband, however, seemed as if he was made to be a father. The oldest of five, he helped raise his younger siblings, and the rhythms of rocking baby, changing baby, and feeding baby came back to him like muscle memory. *He* is a natural. He has yet to read one parenting book and somehow seems to always know exactly what to do. I watched in awe and envy as he, with efficient choreography and playful execution, fathered our child. He won a genuine smile from her when she wasn't even a week old. He made up songs and peekaboo games. He knew how to burp her just right and, to his own benefit, could fall back asleep immediately after being woken by a cry in the middle of the night. *How is this so easy for him?* I thought to myself. *Where did he learn this stuff?*

Still, in those hazy, confounding days of early parenthood, I was brimming with all the satisfaction of a dream come true, a buried hope breaking forth into the light of day. I'd come to the end of anxiety, I thought. My hopes had been realized. I was finally going to be happy.

Children often serve as a vessel for our most existential longings; at least that's what Plato believed.[4] For the nonreligious, offspring can become a stand-in for the hope of immortality. If death is the end, then kids make us feel as if we will live on somehow. If the divine is a hoax, then parenting becomes a type of religion unto itself, a deep source of meaning and purpose. It's a lot of pressure for a seven-pound squealing infant who is just learning to eat and poop.

For the religious, however, the motivation to have children is based on the premise that we know God's *best* blessing through our descendants. "Children are a heritage from the LORD, offspring a reward from him. Like arrows in the hands of a warrior are children born in one's youth. Blessed is the man whose quiver is full of them" (Ps. 127:3–5). Some Christian leaders even advocate for having large families as an apologetics tactic. Writes pastor and author Kevin DeYoung:

> Here's a culture war strategy conservative Christians should get behind: have more children and disciple them like crazy. Strongly consider having more children than you think you can handle...Do you want to rebel against the status quo? Do you want people to ask you for a reason for the hope that is in you (1 Peter 3:15)? Tote your brood of children through Target.[5]

The problem with this approach is that many faithful Christian couples cannot have lots of children. And for those that can, much of the time the person "handling" and "toting" the children is primarily the mother, especially in conservative evangelical circles. The value of feminine domesticity was imparted to me by men and women alike. It always seemed acceptable for me to pursue my vocational gifts and professional desires as long as I didn't have children. As soon as I became a mother, though, the best thing I could do with my life was redirect all my energy to the home. My husband, however, was free to explore any of his goals and interests, kids or no kids. In this model, the good Christian husband is one who goes out and earns money for his family. And the good Christian wife is one who stays home with her children. If she was uninterested in the tasks of homemaking, then it was a sign that she lacked humility and servanthood. If she was drawn to work outside the home, then she was a usurper, hungry for power or money or recognition.

Staying home with children may very well be a good and wise choice for many women. But the idea that godly womanhood is inextricably linked to domesticity is more of a middle-class, Victorian-era construct than a biblical mandate. Prior to the Industrial Revolution, the home was the center of industry for both men and women. Families didn't need as much money because husbands, wives, children, and extended family worked together to make or grow what they needed to survive. In fact, there are magazine articles from the early nineteenth century that champion the trait of domesticity in men![6]

But as families moved to urban centers, and opportunities for wage labor became more widespread, it made more economic sense for men to work at separate labor sites like the factory, dock, railroad, or business office to earn an income. Women—particularly white, economically advantaged women—stayed home and tended to the children and household chores. This middle-class convention became a social paradigm that persisted all the way through to the age of *Leave It to Beaver* and *Ozzie and Harriet* in the 1950s and 1960s. The masculine ideal became husband as the strong, skilled provider; and the feminine ideal became wife as the loving, nurturing homemaker.

Christians have always read Scripture through the cultural lens of their time. Preachers and teachers often overlaid this Victorian ideal onto every Bible passage about marriage. But this stringent commitment to masculine leadership as wage earner and feminine submission as homemaker left me with a lot of unanswered questions. What about Mary, whom Jesus praised for shirking her household responsibilities to sit at his feet and learn in the rabbinic style typically reserved for men? What about Priscilla and Aquila, a couple who seem equally invested in the work of the church? Why were preachers always doing interpretive backflips to explain how the virtuous woman of Proverbs 31 could possibly be allowed to buy a field or sell sashes to merchants if she was not supposed to be working outside the home?

In 2023, while most of the country has accepted that it's possible for men and women to share equally in both economic and domestic responsibilities, many churches still lag behind on their imposed expectations for women. I'm beginning to feel that this does a disservice both to mothers and to fathers. Families should be able to decide for themselves what makes the most sense for them in terms of gifts, interests, and economic needs. No Victorian-era paradigm of masculinity and femininity should force one person into bearing the full weight of financial provision alone. Nor should the tasks of managing a household be one person's obligation. There are many ways to raise a family, homemake, and provide. The healthiest families I know see each aspect of family life as a shared responsibility, with its various functions ebbing and flowing as seasons and circumstances change.

Having children certainly requires sacrifice. Often one or both spouses need to set aside some professional or ministerial goals for a time, as the kids require an extra measure of energy and attention. But the expectation that a woman, if she is truly godly, should gladly set aside all other interests in the name of homemaking creates a culture of shame around motherhood that most men will never fully understand. There is nothing more lonely and disempowering than feeling like the charge of raising children is yours alone.

I'll never forget sitting in a meeting with a male colleague a few weeks before my first daughter was born. He was interested in whether or not I was planning on quitting my job after I had the baby so I could be a stay-at-home mom.

"Well, I have a friend just down the road who wants to babysit for us," I told him. "I can go visit and nurse the baby a couple times a day. I'd like to try and keep working…see how it goes."

He smiled condescendingly at me. "Sure, I know you think that now," he said. "But just wait until you hold that baby in your arms. Wait until you lay eyes on her. I bet you'll change your mind."

Psalm 84:7 tells us that followers of God move "from strength to strength." Sometimes in my life, I feel like I move from shame to shame.

When I was first married and didn't want children right away, I felt guilty that my maternal inclinations seemed stymied. Later, when I did want kids but couldn't get pregnant, I felt guilty that my body could not reproduce on command. Then when I got pregnant, I felt guilty that I'd abandoned the sacred sisterhood of infertility. When I had a baby, I felt guilty for my joy when I knew so many others who could not experience parenthood.

And now that I have a four-year-old and a toddler and the wide-eyed wonder of those first few weeks of motherhood has faded into the everyday grind of homemaking, I feel guilty that I'm not over-the-moon delighted with all the tasks associated with caring for children. I'm embarrassed that the anxiety I experienced during pregnancy did not magically evaporate once the girls were born, that my grief for the lost babies was not eclipsed by the births of healthy babies. I feel embarrassed that motherhood is so hard for me, that I struggle sometimes to engage my children with energy and creativity.

In the spectrum of human shame, "mommy guilt" is perhaps one of the hardest to shake. Shame, for me, usually seems rooted in the idea that there is always something I should be doing that I'm not, something I should be wanting that I don't, something I should be being, but I am not. Shame tells me *this* is not good enough. *Here* is not good enough. *Now* is not good enough. *I* am not good enough. Some perfect version of myself and my life awaits me in the future, if only I can find it. If only I shape up.

Few things in life are as disorienting or shameful as experiencing the disappointment of a dream. I'm not talking about a dream that's been thwarted or unrealized. I'm talking about a dream that's been fully reached and yet doesn't achieve the heights of happiness you assumed it would. Harvard University psychologist Dr. Tal Ben-Shahar refers to this experience as "arrival fallacy," a term he coined to describe the disillusionment that comes when the thing we always wanted doesn't deliver on the promise to make us happy. He notes that the level of dopamine in our brains rises when we anticipate a goal or desire. We are literally hardwired to take pleasure in the pursuit of a dream. Once the goal is reached, that dopamine, and the feeling of pleasure it brings, crashes.[7]

"Be careful what you wish for—lest it come true," goes the old saying, originally attributed to Aesop of the famed fables. Perhaps the caution is not for the wishing but rather for the assumptions— the confidence that every blessing arrives pain-free, that every desire is unblemished, that the reward is always equal to the effort, that the return on investment is always satisfying.

It came as a huge shock to me that motherhood, something I wanted so much, could turn out to be so taxing. So exhausting. Is this what it means to be a mother? To feel like your heart is beating outside of your body and you'll never get it back behind your rib cage? To spend your life cleaning up the messes of other people? To constantly be moving: lifting, squatting, wiping, holding? My arms have ached for four years now. I am exhausted, not in an "I just need a nap" kind of way. I am weary at the molecular level.

When I was struggling with infertility, I resented my friends who complained of exhaustion and diaper blowouts and tantrums. I would have given anything to be up all night with a baby, to clean up after a baby, to be worn thin by a baby. So, when I finally did become a mom, I couldn't fathom how I'd possibly managed to misunderstand myself so egregiously. Had I been foolish or irresponsible to pursue motherhood? A series of lies swirled around in my head: If I was truly spiritually fit, I'd be more energetic. If I was a sacrificial person, I'd rise to the occasion. If my love was stronger, I'd feel less depleted. If I was grounded in Christ, I'd be happy.

Anne Morrow Lindbergh, in her classic book of meditations on motherhood, *Gift from the Sea*, writes, "The bearing, rearing, feeding and educating of children, the running of a house with its thousand details; human relationships with their myriad of pulls—woman's normal occupations in general run counter to creative life, or contemplative life, or saintly life."[8]

I can see where Lindbergh is coming from. I've often felt that motherhood might make me lose my book contract. And more than once I've thought it might even make me lose my religion.

Sometimes I wonder what it would be like—in this competitive, productivity-driven culture—if we did not see our exhaustion as a sign of failure or inadequacy. What if, instead, we saw it as a sign that we are doing something right? Depletion is an indication that you've given your all to an endeavor, that you've put your whole heart into it. It is not necessarily an indication of your inability to balance life's demands or work efficiently. To show up for your children—in your imperfection and in your depletion—is enough.

Parenthood required a creativity of love that was all new to me, a sainthood that was exacting and unfamiliar. As my friend Taylor puts it, to impose a limit upon oneself in the name of servanthood is a practice beautifully akin to the monastic life. In this way, Lindbergh's sentiment may be missing the opportunities that parenthood presents. While motherhood is not the *only* way God shapes women spiritually, it certainly serves as a powerful path into new forms of contemplation, invention, imagination, and artistry.[9]

Motherhood is indeed a role worth investing in, bodily, mentally, and emotionally. It requires you to dig deep, to find places in your heart you didn't know existed, to tap into wells of energy you didn't know were there. If I am tired, it is because I've tried. I've tried with all my might to be a good mother. And I think, most days, I am.

The apostle Paul writes in 1 Timothy 2:15, "But women will be saved through childbearing—if they continue in faith, love and holiness with propriety." Patriarchal systems have used this verse for centuries to subjugate women into believing that their only role was to reproduce, that they achieved salvific purpose only through marriage and motherhood. It has been seen as a reminder of the curse they incurred upon themselves, as Eve did when she allowed herself to be deceived by Satan.

But New Testament scholar N. T. Wright suggests that we may have misunderstood that passage. He says this about childbirth: "[Paul] offers the assurance that, though childbirth is indeed difficult, painful, and dangerous, often the most testing moment in a woman's life, this is not a curse which must be taken as a sign of God's displeasure. God's salvation is promised to all, women and men, who follow Jesus in faith, love, holiness and prudence. And that salvation is promised to those who contribute to God's creation through childbearing, just as it is to everyone else."[10]

What if this passage is simply a declaration that God will sustain you, through whatever exhaustion, frustration, and depletion you experience, whether it be ministry, motherhood, or a career?

Parenthood is a challenge that never stands alone. It is always accompanied by an array of complicating conditions. We all come into parenthood with different strengths and weaknesses. Some of us have supportive partners and family systems while others do not. Some are constrained by financial scarcity. Some are balancing the burden of being a caretaker to other family members. Some have children with unique health challenges, and some parents are dealing with health challenges of their own. We bring our grief to parenting. We bring our doubt. We bring our relational brokenness and our own childhood traumas. I know that there is a lot of solidarity to be found in the "mommy blog" world. But I get a little nervous when any mother tries to give another mother advice or tell her exactly how something should be done. Idolizing celebrity moms, whose online presentations are highly curated, can create the illusion that perfection in parenting can be achieved if only we were better, if only we tried harder.

My girls came to me at a time in life that was racked with grief. My sister died suddenly when my oldest daughter was just eight months old. My youngest was born almost two years later after two more miscarriages. In some ways I feel like I've raised them in the aftermath of an atom bomb. I wanted to give them my best, but my heart was shattered and my mind a mess. I want them to know a mother who smiles and laughs readily. But they have known a mother who cries often and is easily overwhelmed.

Still, this fact remains undeniable—God has sustained me.

The blessing of parenthood hasn't always fit as comfortably as I thought it would. The emotional prosperity gospel loves to classify things as either good or bad, desirable or disagreeable. But most things in life don't fit into these neat categories. This weary and wondrous way of motherhood is a great mystery to me. Sometimes I lay my heavy head on the pillow at night and wonder how to characterize my life. *Is it good? Is it hard? Do I struggle with it? Do I love it?* The answer, it seems, is yes to all of the above.

Sometimes I think the reason parents aren't more honest about the hardships of raising children is because the experience of parenthood can feel like one of life's greatest paradoxes. How is it possible that the most exhausting season of life is also the most exhilarating? How can a tiny human who squeezes so much energy out of you also fill you with so much love? Despite the fact that I often feel ill-suited for motherhood, I am always astounded by how miraculous it is to be the parent of these two beautiful girls.

Sometimes, I'll slip into the bed where my youngest is sleeping. We'll be lying belly to belly, her breath on my neck, and I am certain in those moments that I have the whole world in my arms. She—this little spirit-animating body—is everything. To see life through the eyes of a child once more is an incredible gift. The privilege of parenting within community—with the help of extended family and friends—has been a beautiful experience. I've bonded with my mother-in-law, Jean, who raised five children, as I sought her wisdom and advice. Babysitters who help us with the girls have become lifelong friends. Co-parenting with Tim has been a joy. His "play ethic" certainly rivals the strength of his work ethic. He has a way of finding the fun even in the most ordinary tasks.

I have to trust that there is grace in this season, that there is ample inspiration to be found in the disarray of my life at the present moment, that the pressures of parenthood may call me into a haggard but holy form of sainthood. I cannot assume that the life I want is waiting for me just around the corner—when I am finally able to sleep through the night without someone crying for me, when the kids are at last able to buckle themselves in the car and clean up their own messes. Life is now. I am worn thin because I am offering myself to a million tiny, mundane, beautiful, and wholly necessary demands.

It is incorrect to say that parenthood is right for everyone, that to be a mother is God's highest calling. It is indeed *a* high calling. But I'm not sure you can create hierarchies of ministry, determine which stations in life add more value to the kingdom. The Bible doesn't seem to do this, so I assume God doesn't either. I was not meant to be a mother any more than I was meant to be a missionary or an aid worker or a writer. It is simply a responsibility that I stepped into, a labor I said yes to—that God said yes to. And I am grateful beyond words for it.

In Luke 11, Jesus is teaching a crowd of people when a woman interrupts him and cries out, "Blessed is the mother who gave you birth and nursed you." No doubt, motherhood was as highly revered in Jesus' religious culture as it is in ours. But Jesus' response is surprising. He replies to her, "Blessed rather are those who hear the word of God and obey it" (Luke 11:27, 28). He challenges the excessive veneration of motherhood and highlights what is undoubtably Mary's most exemplary quality: her obedience. Author Kaitlyn Schiess observes that here, Christ demonstrates that he esteems faithfulness in women more than he esteems their fertility.[11] Our calling is simply to say *yes* to God, no matter what he lays before us.

Faithfulness requires stamina. Most things that are worth doing well will thoroughly exhaust you. There is no hack for easy parenting. Any life that is filled with love is likely to be equal parts joy, frustration, sadness, pain, and delight. If a human being is the object of our affection, they are likely to wreak some form of havoc in our lives, no matter their character or intention. Our aching arms are not an indication that we are weak. Rather, they are a sign that we have embraced humanity. Our shoulders throb not because we are feeble but because the burden of love is a heavy one. Heavy and worthwhile. But there is good news.

God will sustain you.

I always knew childbirth would be difficult. What I mean is, I knew labor would be painful. I'd watched enough television to know screaming was part of the deal.

What I wasn't counting on was how difficult wanting children and not having them would be. How difficult pregnancy and miscarriage would be. How difficult being a mother would be.

After the curse is pronounced over the snake in Genesis chapter 3, the woman learns of the consequences of her own sin: "I will make your pains in childbearing very severe; with painful labor you will give birth to children" (v. 16).

Old Testament scholar John Walton points out that most of our modern-day translations of this text have failed to capture the heart of what God is saying here. That first word for "pains" is the

Hebrew word *itstsabon*. Nouns and verbs from the same root word are used to refer to agony, hardship, worry, and grief. It is meant to indicate mental or psychological anguish more than physical pain.

Moreover, the word that is often translated as "childbearing"—*heron*—is really better understood as conception. Walton therefore believes that the first half of this verse actually describes the anxiety and grief women will experience through the entire process of wanting to conceive, of being pregnant, and giving birth.

In this way, a woman's labor to bring something beautiful into the world mirrors the man's labor to draw life-sustaining fruit from the ground. Genesis names the curse as hostile to our efforts to live, to breathe, to give life.

Failure to be fertile, to conceive, to give birth. Failure to "thrive" as a mother…all of these gnaw at the identity and self-confidence of women, especially if they've been told their whole lives the essence of womanhood is motherhood. If I couldn't conceive or couldn't hack it as a mother, was I even a woman at all?

But Genesis 3 tells me that I am no failure, that parenthood has been arduous from the beginning. God sees our pain and speaks to it. The struggle is not a sign of inadequacy but rather a sign of resistance! We are undermining the fall when we seek to give life, and the curse will wage war against us at every turn. And, as Paul wrote, God is our Savior and sustainer through it all.

There is absolutely dignity in diaper changing. While conservative Christianity may have overglorified the role of motherhood, capitalism, conversely, has a way of making us feel that if there isn't monetary value attached to something, then it's not worthwhile. Since the advent of wage labor, the work of the home has been marginalized as secondary, as mindless, as commonplace. But there is nothing commonplace about caretaking the life of another—whether you do it as a mother, father, sibling, friend, or neighbor. The work we do in service of others as volunteers, as guardians, and as mentors matters whether or not we are paid for it. The creation mandate of Genesis 1 is not a call to *wage* labor. It is a call to labor. Love is a labor, one that is both demanding and beautiful. There is no price tag that could accurately reflect its worth.

Several years ago, when I was reading through the Bible as I was nursing my infant daughter, I counted all the times in Scripture God is compared to a woman in labor or prophetic work is likened to the work women undertake in pregnancy. I counted at least seventeen times that this occurred. What a tender, empathetic choice on God's part to elevate women in this way. What a show of solidarity, an endowment of dignity. God sees us. God's passionate exertion for our redemption is like a woman in labor. A woman in labor is, in a way, like God.

In a world that argues about gender roles and reproductive rights, the bodies of women have too often become battlegrounds. What we grievously fail to recognize in these discourses is how beautifully mysterious motherhood is. For nine months, a body that is not my body is housed within my body. I serve as a host to a new life. An act of love with my husband made it so. Love begets more love. And this love that is mine will require more of me than I know how to give. Even beyond pregnancy and birth, motherhood reminds me that a life lived in service to another will never entirely be *my own*. I surrender control, surrender rest, surrender my own self-directed desires for the sake of another.

This is the exhausting and beautiful work of life unto life, love unto love. This is the work of procreation.

A BLESSING:
Delight

*What do workers gain from their toil? I have seen the burden
God has laid on the human race. He has made everything
beautiful in its time. He has also set eternity in the human
heart; yet no one can fathom what God has done from beginning to end. I know that there is nothing better for people
than to be happy and to do good while they live. That each
of them may eat and drink, and find satisfaction in all their
toil—this is the gift of God.*

—Ecclesiastes 3:9–13

Work. Marriage. Parenthood. These are the good and noble
endeavors that were first touched by the curse. The pronouncement of Genesis 3 is plain: The woman will groan in childbearing, partners will struggle for power, and the ground of our
labor will produce thorns and thistles. These beautiful burdens
have indeed become heavy. Perhaps the greatest tragedy of all is
that even in those rare and wonderful moments when we do yield a
harvest—when love and submission are mutual, when the children
are healthy and safe, and there is good fruit to be found among the

briars and brambles—we still struggle to savor it. We've lost our taste for sweetness, squandered our aptitude for satisfaction.

When you live in the land of bootstraps and endless aspirations, you are always haunted by the hope of something better around the corner. Happier horizons and brighter futures beckon us. There will always be another job that seems more meaningful. There will always be another ministry that appears more important and exciting. There will always be another person you are convinced would have made a better partner. There is always an elusive "someday" when you will feel well-rested, at peace, and proud of yourself.

"If I were to invent a sin to describe what that was—for how I lived—I would not say it was simply that I didn't stop to smell the roses," writes Kate Bowler. "It was the sin of arrogance, of becoming impervious to life itself. I failed to love what was present and decided to love what was possible instead."[1]

It was the crafty Serpent who first spoke to Eve about her lack. His question was a cunning one: "Did God really say, 'You must not eat from any tree in the garden'?" (Gen. 3:1). The inquiry is a strange one because any careful reader of the text knows that God gave the *entire* garden to Adam and Eve to cultivate and enjoy, with boundless beautiful trees to eat from and savor. There was only one tree that he told them not to eat from. And yet the Serpent, in his craftiness, planted a seed of doubt, causing Eve to ponder, perhaps for the first time, her deprivation. God had provided so much sweetness, yet suddenly the Serpent made her feel swindled. Perhaps Eve's most profound failure was not her inability to recognize deceit, but rather her inability to recognize delight.

And so, that depravity has woven its sad thread through the human story ever since. We earnestly pursue the right script or the perfect system that will make happiness the paradigm and sadness an anomaly. We are most comfortable with neat, tidy categories—with blessings that are pristine in every way. It's hard to imagine that anything good could also be hard. We struggle to wrap our arms around an experience or a love that is both draining and invigorating, hurtful and healing. So often, the beautiful bits of our lives are lost in the messiness of it all. And wonder is drowned out by the din of the ordinary.

I believe it is God's desire to help us recognize and recover that beauty. One of God's most powerful responses to the fall of humankind was Sabbath. Sabbath was not merely a day of rest from the thorny, rocky fields. It was meant to be a day dedicated to the discipline of delight. In this way, the practices of the people of Israel were wildly different from those of surrounding nations. Scholars tell us that many cultures of ancient Mesopotamia saw the seventh day of the week as evil or unlucky. The people of those cultures also rested on the seventh day, but for them the rest was driven by fear because they believed that working on an unlucky day could lead to failure or harmful accidents. The ancient Israelites, however, rested on the seventh day because God had commanded them to. In contrast to its neighbors, Israel saw the seventh day not as one of gloom and doom, but of joy, celebration, comfort, and leisure.[2] It was a day for savoring the loving-kindness of God and the freely given blessings all around us.

The world, for all its brokenness, is still an extraordinarily beautiful and pleasurable place to call home. Contrary to the Serpent's sly suggestion, God did in fact give us an abundant garden with endless groves of magnificent trees—so many of which grow and produce fruit through no effort of our own. There is a God-breathed splendor to the material world. When we consider the elegant design of our physical bodies, the majesty of the land-scape that surrounds us, the glory of the sky above us—we cannot help but marvel at the order, the function, and the artistry of it all. How can we say that creation is anything less than lavish when we contemplate the endless varieties of fruits and flowers in all their alluring detail, diversity, and tastes? God made our tongues to know sweetness, ears to hear music, skin to savor the touch of our loved ones, and eyes to take in the splendor of a sunset. Even our most ordinary days are filled with miracles: the bonds of friendship, love, romance, parental instincts, the creation and enjoyment of art, the making of a home, and the satisfaction of a job well done. The emotional experience of being human is abso-lutely exquisite.

This excess of beauty woven into the fabric of creation leads me to believe one thing: God delights in seeing his children delighted. And it was this delight that the wise writer of Ecclesiastes offered as a solution to the disillusionment he experienced. The sage king Qohelet—after he'd bemoaned the vanity of achievement, lamented the precariousness of wealth, and wept for the inevitabil-ity of death—came to a clear conclusion: "A person can do noth-ing better than to eat and drink and find satisfaction in their own toil. This too, I see, is from the hand of God" (Eccles. 2:24). He goes on, "However many years anyone may live, let them enjoy them all" (11:8).

Qohelet is not the first nor the last to offer delight as an anti-dote to despair. Hedonism is a theory of motivation embraced by both ancient and modern philosophers. Hedonism posits that the only real value or meaning in life is found in the experience of plea-sure and the avoidance of pain. But there is a difference between a wanton, idolatrous form of hedonism and the holy hedonism

68

of Qohelet. Holy hedonism is the insistence that we savor and experience the world as God intended—with dignity. This means we assume the dignity of our fellow humans, of God's creation, and of ourselves. Real joy is meant to be immersive, not distractive. Food was made to be relished not gorged. Sex was made to be mutually enjoyed not exploited. The earth was made to be inhabited not plundered. Humans were made to live in community not empire. Delight in its holiest form is the antithesis of exploitation. It is patient, authentic, and embodied. It is the ennobling of the human experience.

Resistance against the war that the curse wages on our work, marriages, families, and friendships requires a commitment to the art of noticing. It requires us to cultivate a sense of awe. We must attune our hearts to pay attention and value authentic pleasure rather than crude imitations. We must appreciate what our lives actually are rather than be intoxicated with the mythologies of "someday" or "if only." Writes author Cole Arthur Riley, "I think awe is an exercise, both a doing and a being. It is a spiritual muscle of our humanity that we can only keep from atrophying if we exercise it habitually."[3]

When I look back on my life, my moments of purest joy have often been found in the commonplace. My deepest delights have been in the smallness of an ordinary but beautiful existence. A simple cup of cider shared with a group of friends around a campfire. A grueling house renovation project with my husband that turned into an evening of laughter and connection. A surprise winter storm that left us snowed in at home cuddling with our kids and living off ramen noodles and peanut butter sandwiches. A day rescuing fish from a leaky pond, golden treasures flopping around in the muck.

Unplanned. Unexpected. Unearned. To trade my aspirations of achievement, prosperity, and perfection for the taste of an apple, a glimpse of the stars, or a game of imagination with my child is a sacred exchange. I have been wooed by the simple goodness of God. My gaze has been lifted from my own self-importance. I am transfixed by the beauty of the world.

Delight has become a way of life for me. When the world seems to be too much—when the tasks ahead of me seem undoable, when I'm undone by grief, when I am bone-weary and disillusioned—in those moments of acute helplessness, I interrupt my despair with delight. I commit myself to the holy act of noticing. I ask myself, *What good and noble thing has God given me today that I can relish in?* Is it the feel of sunshine on my face? Is it the bounce of my daughter's curls? Is it the warm heartiness of the stew simmering on the stove for dinner? Is it a laugh I will share with my husband about an inside joke? Is it the sound of the spring peepers drifting through the open window? I immerse myself in the beauty of the world, in the hidden graces of my very own life.

This feels like a *true* blessing. Sometimes I think that the greatest apologetic a Christian can offer the world is to be genuinely, entirely present in your life. In a culture that says, "More is more," the great protest of the Christian is to say, "Enough is enough." What if we lingered longer over our meals, sat face-to-face in conversation, hiked out to the beautiful backcountry, learned to play instruments, and spent excessive time gazing at the stars? What if, when that sneaky Serpent comes to us whispering lies about our lack, we looked up at all the glorious apple trees instead? Would not the world have been a different place had only Adam and Eve stopped to savor what *was* instead of what could be?

PART 2

CHAPTER 4

CALLING

(Discover God's Will for Your Life)

"God has a wonderful plan for your life!"

It is 1996-ish and adolescent Amanda is sitting on a hard plywood pew of an outdoor chapel at a Christian summer camp in rural Alabama. My fellow campers and I are furiously taking notes in our camp-issued spiral-bound notebooks as the special speaker tells us tales of David Livingstone, the famed missionary who purportedly brought the gospel to the continent of Africa. Livingstone, a man of deep conviction and undaunted courage, had followed the call of Christ, and it led him to great sacrifice and great adventure. Tears filled my eyes as I heard stories of his encounters with tigers, malaria, and curious locals. By the time the speaker told us that Livingstone had insisted that his heart be buried in Africa, we were all puddles. *This* was a man who had found his *calling*.

"Are *you* at the center of God's will for *your* life?" the speaker asked us, pounding the podium and pointing his finger. "Are you willing to follow God no matter where he leads you?"

Anyone who grew up evangelical is familiar with the concept of calling, this particular purpose God specifically designed for your life based on your unique gifts, talents, and interests. Calling—a critical component of the emotional prosperity gospel—was like a customized blueprint, a wonderful plan and beautiful story God wanted to tell with your life.

Alas, it seemed like it was incumbent upon me to figure out what exactly that wonderful plan was. If God's will had a center, I figured I'd best be in it. I needed to find out what *place* I'd been called to—maybe Africa or an urban neighborhood? I had to discover what *people group* I should serve—perhaps homeless youth or a tribe in the Amazon rain forest? And I needed to know if there was a *position* that God had in mind for me—a teacher or a doctor or a lawyer? This divine Venn diagram, where place, people group, and position all converged—that was the center of God's will. At least it was in my mind.

I'd also heard that God had a *person* picked out for me to marry, a soulmate who would "do life" with me at the center of God's will. "I'm feeling called to pursue you romantically" was an oft-used pickup line on Christian college campuses in the '90s. This certainly created some spiritual and social tension, as sometimes God had "revealed" to one person that they were called to marry someone who had not yet received the same revelation from God.

If attending a Christian college was supposed to help you find your calling—and your soulmate—the endeavor, for me, had failed miserably. I'd changed majors three times and went on only a small handful of dates with guys who were clearly not my soulmate. I had a million things I wanted to do. I was passionate about everything from missions to microloans, social work to songwriting. I wanted to stop human trafficking, stop the AIDS crisis, stop genocide in Darfur, stop gun violence. *I wanted to stop all the things.*

There were lots of methods my peers used for discerning God's will for their lives. These methods ranged from judicious to downright wacky. Some sought the advice of elders or spent hours in prayer. Others flipped through their Bibles, pointing to random verses to see what specific insight could be found. Some laid out some sort of fleece, like Gideon in the Old Testament. Others documented their dreams at night and looked for a pattern.[1]

I took a prudent and practical approach. I spent countless evenings taking aptitude tests and personality assessments. There were plenty to choose from: Myers-Briggs Type Indicator, StrengthsFinder, and a variety of spiritual giftings tests. The S.H.A.P.E. Test (Spiritual Gifts, Heart, Abilities, Personality, Experiences) promises to help you "discover who God made you to be." Last time I checked, the home page of their website bombards you with a bold banner that reads: "Got Purpose?"[2]

Some of the tests told me I should be a counselor. Others said I should work at a museum or be a professor. One indicated I was uniquely designed by God to be a canned goods label maker. The more tests I took, the more opaque God's will became. "Holy Spirit, speak to me through this test!" I would pray. But God's voice remained too still and too small to discern.

Mentors and peers alike told me that the ultimate way of knowing if something was God's will was whether or not you had a peace about it. If you experienced this peace after a decision, it was clearly the right thing to do.

Unfortunately, I didn't have peace about anything. At night, I'd lie in my dorm room listening to old Steven Curtis Chapman records and dreaming about my own *great adventure*. I knew I was going to do amazing things for God, I just didn't know what.

Looking back, it's humbling to think about how much my privileges—my freedom of choice, my mobility, my vocational opportunities—were torturing me. "The standard line is that choice is good for us, that it confers on us freedom, personal responsibility, self-determination, autonomy and lots of other things that don't help when you're standing before a towering aisle of water bottles, paralyzed and increasingly dehydrated, unable to choose," writes journalist Stuart Jeffries.[3] From career day, to the Oreo cookie aisle, to dating apps that allow us to scroll through endless images of potential dating partners, we have been convinced that the perfect job, the perfect snack, the perfect partner is out there somewhere. If we make the right choice, we will be happy.

Jeffries goes on: "Increased choice has created a new problem: the escalation in expectations."[4] Many of us, when our good choices don't produce the level of happiness we expect to experience, end up developing lifelong, searing regrets. Barry Schwartz, author of *The Paradox of Choice*, notes, "This imagined alternative induces you to regret the decision you made, and this regret subtracts from the satisfaction of the decision you made, even if it was a good decision."[5]

I am unhappy, so I must have made the wrong choice, we think to ourselves. *I missed out on my best life.*

Now that I'm older, I've wondered if this obsession we all had as young people with the concept of calling was simply a way for us to deal with the overwhelming choice anxiety and decision fatigue. The great hope of the Christian is that God will intervene, reveal his will for your life, eliminate the guesswork, and reinforce his sovereign presence in your life. God will *tell you* what to do. Blessedness can be found at the center of his will. Find your calling and you will be happy.

℃

While Christians in the late twentieth century were hemming and hawing about finding their calling, the self-help and wellness movement was busy building a multimillion-dollar industry. Many of the self-help books that show up on the *New York Times* Best Sellers list these days echo the ideology of the New Thought movement of the early nineteenth century. They insist that we can control our outcomes through the power of positive thinking. You are limited by only your lack of imagination. Listen to the divine voice within and embrace your own deservedness. You are entitled to a beautiful and wonderful life.

It's an appealing notion that we can pep-talk ourselves into blessedness, that adventures await us if we only have faith. "Decide what you want. Believe you can have it. Believe you deserve it. Believe it's possible for you,"[6] readers are instructed in Rhonda Byrne's enormously popular book *The Secret*, which has sold more than thirty million copies. It's certainly a far cry from the ancient Greek understanding of happiness as merely happenstance, fate, or a whim of favor from the gods.

Elizabeth Gilbert, whose book *Eat, Pray, Love* remained on the *New York Times* Best Sellers list for 187 weeks, writes:

> Happiness is the consequence of personal effort. You fight for it, strive for it, insist upon it, and sometimes even travel around the world looking for it…You have to participate

relentlessly in the manifestations of your own blessings...
You must make a mighty effort to keep swimming upward
into that happiness forever, to stay afloat on top of it.[7]

"You are perfect," writes another best-selling author, Jen Sincero. "And your job is to be as you as you can be. This is why you're here. To shy away from who you truly are would leave the world you-less...Do not deny the world its one and only chance to bask in your brilliance."[8] In our world, personal passion has become the new moral compass. Self-discovery is an ethical imperative. The greatest virtue is to unleash your most authentic self and chase the thing you find most exhilarating.

Byrne, in her follow-up book titled *The Power*, writes, "You are the creator of your life. You are the writer of your life story. You are the director of your life movie."[9] The world is our stage, and we are the main character. Timothy Ferriss, author of *The 4-Hour Workweek*, another bestseller, writes, "Excitement is the more practical synonym for happiness, and it is precisely what you should strive to chase. It is the cure-all."[10] According to Ferriss, "The opposite of happiness is—here's the clincher—boredom."[11]

I'd venture to guess that most of our ancestors would have been perplexed by this hunger for excitement and adventure. I imagine many of them longed for a quiet and boring life, a life free of marauding warlords or plagues or dangerous quests. It is the hard times that call for heroic deeds, and they were likely weary of tumult and peril. It is perhaps the height of privilege to look at a man like William Wallace (otherwise known as Braveheart), a guy who was hanged, drawn, and quartered, with envy. Nevertheless, the hunger for the thrill of danger is real and powerful. In 2014, iconic fashion entrepreneur Tory Burch told the graduating class of Babson College, "If it doesn't scare you, you're not dreaming big enough."[12]

Christians may think that they are above all this talk of deservedness, vanity, and thrill-seeking. But we yearn for excitement and importance as much as the next person. We long to know our lives matter, that we can change the world if we really want to. We fear boredom. We chafe at anonymity.

John Eldredge, author of the hugely popular Christian book *Wild at Heart*, writes, "I'm convinced that adventure, with all its requisite danger and wildness, is a deeply spiritual longing written into the soul of man. Does that surprise you, hearing that adventure is a *spiritual* longing given to us by God?"[13] He describes the ideal Christian life in this way: "There is a life that few men know…a life so rich and free, so dangerous and yet so exhilarating in its impact that if you knew now what you *could* have, you would sell everything to find it."[14]

Beloved author Donald Miller writes in his book *A Million Miles in a Thousand Years*, "Once you live a good story, you get a taste for a kind of meaning in life, and you can't go back to being normal; you can't go back to meaningless scenes stitched together by the forgettable thread of wasted time."[15] Rachel Hollis, who built a Christian self-help empire after her book *Girl, Wash Your Face* took the world by storm, writes, "This is your life. You are meant to be the hero of your own story."[16]

I don't fault any of these authors for encouraging people to think outside the box, to make an effort to spend time and energy on worthy pursuits. But I worry that some of us may have begun to believe that the ultimate tragedy would be to live an ordinary life. To be normal. To be anything less than a victor of mythic proportions. I had couched my own longing for significance and adventure within a Christian framework. I anointed my ambitions as holy, declared my pursuit of happiness and meaning to be a divine expedition for the cause of Christ.

I had to find my own adventure, my own purpose. I had to find my *calling*.

My saving grace in those uncertain years of evangelical adolescence was the patient levelheadedness of my parents. They never really bought into the whole narrative about God having a specific plan for your life that you somehow had to miraculously discern. For them, character formation was more important than a ten-year or twenty-year plan. They told me to just use wisdom and make the best decisions I could. They told me I didn't have to have my whole life figured out just yet, that I could simply take the next right step and see what happened. And they told me that there were probably lots of nice Christian guys out there who would make perfectly good husbands. I trusted them, but I was still nervous.

My senior year I finally decided I'd do a postgraduate internship with three different missions organizations based in southern India. During a spring break trip to Chennai for tsunami relief work, I'd fallen in love with the people and the ministry there. The plan was for me to start in Chennai, working with the leaders of Word for the World to develop partnership and fundraising opportunities in the United States. Then, I'd move to Hyderabad to teach English to a group of students at Ashirvad School, a home and learning center for kids and widows who had been impacted by HIV. Finally, I'd end up in Bangaluru, supporting teachers at a resource center for rescued child laborers. These were all Indian-led organizations, so I was excited about the cultural immersion and offering my newly acquired skills to their ministries.

Additionally, as divine Providence would have it, I started dating someone I was convinced was "God's best" for me just one day before walking across the graduation stage. He, too, was interested in missions work. I'd found my calling *and* my soulmate. I finally had a sense of peace. I'd checked all the boxes just in the nick of time.

I'll never forget the moment the plane landed in India, the tires screeching on the sizzling tarmac. I was finally here, walking fully in my God-given calling. Descending from the airplane, gripping the handle of my guitar case, my hippie skirt swooshing around my ankles, I smiled as the hot, thick Indian air hit me like a wall of steam. I breathed in the nighttime that smelled heavily of smog and faintly of jasmine, shedding a well-executed tear, my eyes lifted heavenward to my Savior. I fancied myself the picture of a young, mission-minded, gospel-driven zealot—a modern-day Lottie Moon. While all my friends were taking cushy office jobs and privileged internships, I was doing something that *actually mattered*. I was sacrificially leaving my boyfriend behind at home (he had one more semester of college to finish). In my mind, we were star-crossed lovers torn apart by altruism, ideals, and self-sacrifice. I imagined the romantic letters we would pen, pining for one another across miles and miles of melancholic ocean. I was perfectly forlorn, walking in the solemn and resolute footsteps of all the great missionaries that had gone before me. This was *my* great adventure. They might as well begin writing the movie script about my amazing life.

Fast-forward three months and I'm sitting on a plastic stool in the back alley of the mission school compound, my knees up to my chin and my arms crossed under my dupatta shawl, while three Indian women gather around me, chattering at each other in Telugu, lathering my hair with some sticky coconut concoction so they can begin combing the infestation of lice out of my hair.

It turns out, even missionaries have bad days.

I'm not talking about the romantic kind of bad days, the idealistic kind of suffering for Jesus we imagine we'll experience at the center of God's will. I'm talking about fantastically uninspiring days. I'm talking about the annoyingly mundane days, or days where tiny calamities disrupt our best-laid plans. I'm talking about the everyday inconveniences and apprehensions that follow you all the way from America to Chennai to Hyderabad to Bangaluru. I'm talking about the days of insecurity and self-doubt. It turns out, wherever I go, *I* go with me.

Once I'd gotten over the novelty and the photo ops, I was frustrated by the behavior of my students, mad that the widow who cleaned my room kept rearranging my stuff, and tired of walking three blocks to a phone booth to call my boyfriend, who, after three months apart, frankly just didn't seem to be that into me anymore.

I spent a lot of time being uncomfortable. It was hot. I missed consistent internet. I didn't love Tamil soap operas. People didn't get my sense of humor. A bad motorbike burn and subsequent infection sent me to the hospital and left me unable to walk for a week. I wasn't able to contribute as much as I wanted to the ministries because I wasn't fluent in Tamil or Telugu. I was culturally exhausted and broken by loneliness at times. I was bored. At night, when the electricity would go out, I'd sit at the kitchen table and watch the wick on my small candle slowly burn down, thinking of all the things I was missing out on back home. It took a while for my stomach to adjust to the food. I once had an amoeba that made me so sick I wished for death and started writing my will. Turns out, suffering for Jesus means spending a lot of time near a toilet. The whole venture was a lot less sexy than I expected it to be. The movie of my life would require a lot of editing: Yelling out English verb conjugations at unruly students and puking up potato curry isn't exactly blockbuster material.

No, I didn't need a life of ease or profit. No, I didn't need health and wealth. But I did want to feel like all this sacrifice was at least making a difference. The sense of calling that was so palpable on the plane ride over to India seemed to be slipping from my grasp a mere three months in. Where was my great adventure? Where was this incredible story I was supposed to be telling with my life?

It wasn't always the responsibility of the individual to write their own story and craft their own identity. In generations past, a person's sense of self was dictated by external forces—the family or clan they belonged to, their position within the socioeconomic sphere, the land they grew up on, or their birth order or marital status. These social and communal components determined a person's place in the world and how they experienced belonging, meaning, and purpose. Societies of the past tended to think collectively as a group, rather than individually.

Some historians say that this all began to change for the Western world in the aftermath of the Black Death in the 1340s, an epidemiological disaster sometimes referred to as the Great

Mortality. It is estimated that anywhere from 30 to 60 percent of the population of Europe and parts of Asia and North Africa perished in this pandemic. Death by the bubonic plague was excruciating. Accounts from that era reveal that when people witnessed how quickly victims would succumb after developing the telltale symptoms of swollen glands and black boils, an "every man for himself" mentality swept the continent. Husbands abandoned wives, mothers abandoned children, and doctors and ministers abandoned their stations.[17] Death made no differentiation between peasant and king, priest and pauper.

Almost every philosophical idea that emerged in the centuries after this terrifying and tumultuous time period emphasized the rights, reasoning, and spirituality of every individual person no matter their status in life. Labor shortages due to the Great Mortality meant workers could demand higher wages and better treatment from their overlords. The scarcity of clergymen—plus the invention of the printing press—led to people taking more personal ownership of their religious beliefs and habits. The Reformation challenged the ecclesiastical hierarchy of the Catholic Church. The Enlightenment, with its emphasis on liberty, democracy, religious tolerance, and opposition to the institution of the monarchy, swept the world. People began to feel truly empowered and entitled to certain rights, as if they had real agency over their own destiny, perhaps for the first time in history.

In the 1480s, a twenty-four-year-old Italian named Giovanni Pico della Mirandola wrote *Oration on the Dignity of Man*, a public discourse that became the landmark rhetorical work of the Renaissance period of humanism. In it he imagined God speaking to human beings about their personal autonomy: "We have made thee neither of heaven nor of earth, neither mortal nor immortal, so that with freedom of choice and with honor, as though the maker and molder of thyself, thou mayest fashion thyself in whatever shape thou shalt prefer."[18]

We are indeed makers and molders of ourselves. Self-actualization is a moral obligation. Writes contemporary Canadian philosopher Charles Taylor, "There is a certain way of being human that is my way. I am called upon to live my life in this way, and not in imitation of anyone else's. But this gives a new importance of being true to myself. If I am not, I miss the point of my life, I miss what being human is for *me*."[19] Family, status, and institutions no longer tell us who we are. *We* determine *who* we are. We write our own narratives, make our own meaning. Author Alan Noble observes, "Self-discovery is our contemporary hero's journey."[20]

But this pursuit of personal meaning seems to be taking its toll. Psychological researchers recently surveyed more than eight thousand people and found that those who indicated they were *searching* for meaning had lower levels of overall life satisfaction and happiness.[21] In spite of the fact that modern Americans have unprecedented freedom of choice, extraordinary vocational mobility, and unparalleled opportunities, we seem to be collectively uneasy and unhappy. Anxiety, depression, and suicidal ideation are all on the rise.[22] While a wide array of stressors may be contributing to this, Barry Schwartz notes that some studies suggest one significant cause: the self-blame that ensues when you feel like you've failed yourself with the choices you've freely made and the identity you've created of your own accord.[23] Agency comes with a massive amount of pressure. When things in life don't go your way, not only do you feel unhappy; you feel shame.

In 1940, only 20 percent of men and 11 percent of women

agreed with the statement "I am an important person." Fifty years later, in 1990, 62 percent of men and 66 percent of women agreed with that same statement.[24] A sense of self-dignity is a beautiful thing. But a growing sense of self-importance can sometimes descend into self-obsession. When hyperindividualism, consumerism, and identity crafting collide, we end up thinking an awful lot about one thing: *ourselves.*

I wonder sometimes if for Christians, the seemingly spiritual longing to find our calling is less reflective of our desire to honor God, and more indicative of our yearning to simply matter. We want all the contours and details of our lives, the threads that make up our days and years, to weave together into a larger story of significance and importance. I have often struggled to discern the difference between the nudge of the Holy Spirit and the inclinations of my own heart. Often, when I feel a desire to do great things for God, it's simply because *I* want to be great. I want my life to be exciting. I want to be admired and remembered.

Choice anxiety. Decision fatigue. The pressure to perform, to prove ourselves *to* ourselves, to others, and to God. Whether you use religious language or cling to the mantras of the self-help movement, the search for meaning is all-consuming. The hero's role is demanding and strenuous. The religion of self-discovery, while it may seem dignifying and liberating on the surface, is really exhausting and enslaving.

What is a calling?

The word "calling" in the Old Testament comes from the Hebrew root *qr'*. It usually means "to name" or "to summon." It is the word used when God gives a name to the heavenly bodies, to the earth, and to the waters. In 1 Samuel 3:3, God calls the little boy Samuel into service with a mysterious voice in the night. In naming, identity is bestowed. In calling, God nominates someone for a task.

In the New Testament, there are many Greek words—like *kalein, legein,* and *phonien*—that are used to denote a name or calling. Here, too, "to call" can mean "to name, identify, summon, or invite."[25] There are a few instances where individuals are given a particular mission. But those orders typically come via the audible voice of God or Jesus Christ himself. Nowhere in the New Testament is the church at large given instructions on how one might discern what specific job they are to take or place they are to live or person they are to marry.

Instead, the Scriptures talk a lot about the *kind* of life we are called into. We are called into fellowship with Christ (see 1 Cor. 1:9). We are called to freedom (see Gal. 5:13). We are called into a shared hope (see Eph. 4:4). We are called to the peace of Christ (see Col. 3:15). We are called into the kingdom and glory of God (see 1 Thess. 2:12). We are called to endure harsh treatment with patience (see 1 Pet. 2:20–21). We are called to give blessings to others, even when they insult us (see 1 Pet. 3:9).

Calling, in the truly biblical sense, is more about character. We are named as God's people, summoned to a purpose greater than ourselves. We are invited into a way of life—a hope, a freedom, a fellowship.

Character shaping sure didn't sound as exciting to twenty-one-year-old Amanda as the great adventure I was promised at the center of God's will. When I moved to India, I'm not sure I found my calling. I did, however, find that my character was being shaped.

The old adage that I "received more than I gave" is cliché, but it perfectly describes my time there. Despite the difficulty of the cultural adjustment, I found India to be a beautiful and engaging country. I was generously invested in by the Indian families that took me in during my stay. Augustine Asir and his family in Chennai mentored me and shared with me all the ins and outs of their daily lives as ministers of the gospel to the marginalized people groups of India's caste system. The local missionaries of Word for the World actually *lived* in the slums, leper colonies, and fishing villages where they ministered. These brave and sacrificial men and women shared the gospel by living alongside those in need, with no pretense of superiority or self-importance.

I was months into my time with the Asirs before I ever learned that Augustine, then in his late sixties, had translated for Billy Graham at his historic evangelistic events and that he had befriended and worked with Mother Teresa. He was basically a Christian celebrity in India, but he and his wife gave up their own bed and slept on the floor of their son's room while I lived with them so that I would be comfortable in the nicest bedroom in their home. He never spoke of his accomplishments. Mostly he bragged on his son, Jim; his daughter, Sharon; his wife, Heera; and the missionaries they led. When I got married three years later, they sent me a gold chain necklace, a gift fathers traditionally give to their daughters on their wedding day. I named my first child, Jane Augustine, in honor of them.

After my time with the Asirs, I moved north to Hyderabad. There I lived with the Chinta family in a three-story building that served as their school and ministry center called Ark Family Ministries. My bedroom was on the first floor and every morning, I woke up to the pitter-patter of the children's feet above me as they readied themselves for the day, completed chores, ate a wholesome breakfast, and prepared to study. The Chintas showed me what it was to truly integrate life and ministry, always flinging their front door open when one of the children came down with a fever, always inviting the caregivers to their table for banana bread and chai. They taught me Telugu, showed me how to make chapatis, and introduced me to Indian cinema.

I learned after I arrived that the price of my plane ticket to Chennai would cover the salary of one Word for the World missionary for an entire year; or cover the annual schooling, housing, and food expenses for three Ark Family kids. The cost of my "great adventure" humbled me. I was no one's savior. The gift of my time in India was not what I accomplished for God, but what he accomplished in me. I learned how to be bored without feeling useless. I learned to "make do"—to adapt to changing environments and be resourceful. I learned to be fully present in a place, even when it wasn't everything I expected it to be. I learned how to look to God, to surrender my future to his loving care. I learned how to be uncomfortable and happy at the same time.

You may have noticed that I am not a missionary. It turns out, that wasn't my calling. I did not become the next David Livingstone or Lottie Moon. And that guy I thought was my soulmate? We broke up. I married Tim instead.

"God will order your steps." I no longer believe that God is playing some cosmic guessing game with us. I believe he protects our path, that somehow his perfect will mysteriously interacts with our imperfect will, and our stories are written. We make the best decisions we can, but we can't always control our outcomes. Some-times life leads us down a road we wouldn't have chosen for our-selves. We are often met with trials, heartache, and, God forbid, boredom.

There's nothing wrong with wanting a good life. And there's nothing wrong with wanting a life that feels purposeful, excit-ing even. The problem is that most of our preferred containers of meaning—work, marriage, ministry—will at some point fail to bring us that coveted sense of significance. So much of life is mun-dane. Ordinary. Just because something is boring doesn't mean it's not important. Just because something stops being person-ally fulfilling doesn't mean it's not worth doing. Just because you aren't receiving accolades doesn't mean you aren't successful. Just because you aren't happy all the time doesn't mean you've made a bad choice.

Most people end up spending much of their lives doing things they never identified as their calling. Life presents us with needs we can't always anticipate. We care for children born with health challenges. We take a second job to pay bills when a financial crisis hits. We move in with aging parents. We spend months in cancer wards or physical therapy. Circumstances out of our control propel us into narratives that are not nearly as exciting and romantic as we'd dreamed. Sometimes we end up playing supporting roles in someone else's story of heroism.

I used to think it was a sin to do something ordinary or boring with my life. Even now, when I am occupied by everyday tasks (like laundry, playdates, or grocery shopping), I feel the disappointed gaze of a God who I imagined wanted *so much more* for my life.

There is a saying I learned from my Indian friends that is often used in business transactions: "Do the needful." The phrase is essentially a request that you do what is necessary as it relates to a certain task. It expresses trust that you will be responsible with the request, that you will be faithful with what is required of you.

Sometimes I wish that all those people who told me I needed to do something grand and adventurous with my life had told me that so much of life is simply doing the needful. And that's okay. It is, in fact, quite beautiful. While it might be easier and more exciting to follow your inner longings, to pack up and passionately pursue some grand adventure, sometimes you don't. Because life and virtue beckon you to stay. To serve. To do the needful. To be faithful to what is required of you.

Calling, it seems, is whatever is in front of you. It is an invitation to be present. It summons us to love, to hope, to be at peace. It is a challenge to simply *be* rather than to *be significant.* A calling is not to be discerned, but to be lived. We do hard things, even bold things, but not because we want to be important. Not because we need to be the protagonist of some grand narrative. We do these things because they are necessary. Because they are the right thing to do. We do them because of love.

What I believe, and hope, is that God calls us to a higher anthropology than the self-indulgent schema of the modern self-help movement and the doctrine of self-discovery. When God calls us, he names us as beloved, gives us a purpose. Dignity is bestowed by him. Our value is not earned but is freely given. We have nothing to prove. His story is ours, and it is enough. There is beauty in simplicity, in ordinariness, and in faithfulness. God's sovereignty mysteriously interacts with our own choices. He guards our steps and secures our future.

And so, we don't have to hustle. We don't have to live in fear of making the wrong choice. We are already found, and we already have an identity. We don't have to be the hero. We are free to enjoy where the road of life takes us—its seasons of adventure, its seasons of stillness, its moments of both notoriety and anonymity.

To me, this is a life of rest. It is a story of grace and trust. This, to me, sounds like *true* freedom.

CHAPTER 5

COMMUNITY

(Share Life Together)

One of the greatest privileges of my very privileged life was the community of faith I experienced growing up. When I was a kid, my family and I were surrounded by loving friends and mentors, by people of faith who saw the world the same way we did. Christian community, for us, felt like it was already built into our lives because my dad always worked at a Christian college; his colleagues became his friends, and their kids became our friends. When we were young, my sister and I attended a Christian elementary school where we learned Bible stories set to song and pledged our allegiance to the Christian flag. We were in church almost every Sunday and, as we got older, participated in youth group on Wednesday nights. And Sunday nights. And the occasional Friday night.

The days of my childhood and adolescence were filled with playdates, potlucks, vacation Bible schools, youth retreats, summer camps, Christian rock concerts, Sunday school, and discipleship groups. There was always something to do and somewhere to go, always someone we could turn to if we needed help. When we were sick, there were casseroles delivered. When our friends were sick, we delivered the casseroles.

After graduating from high school, I chose to go to a Christian college myself, and so that conveyor belt of Christian community kept coming my way. My professors became my mentors and my dormmates became my best friends. They walked with me through all those apprehensive years of identity formation, through the nail-biting and decision-making about my future. My college girl-friends and I cried on one another's shoulders through breakups and were bridesmaids in one another's weddings.

I suppose you could say my life was a pristine product of the '80s and '90s Christian subculture. That subculture was a community of belonging for me, of belovedness. And though there is no doubt that my faith community brought much happiness to my growing-up experience, I now see that the picture it painted of community was incomplete. Almost all my friends had a life circumstance similar to mine: middle-class, white, evangelical. We'd felt a gravitational pull toward one another due to our common experiences, similar likes and dislikes. There were certainly personality differences, but our worldviews were effortlessly compatible, so it was easy to converse, to relate, and to share life.

When I became an adult—when community was no longer built in and I had to build it for myself—I was confronted with some hard questions. I never realized how homogeneous my community was until I landed in a foreign country and suddenly was surrounded by people who didn't look like me or talk like me. In India, I lived and worked with Christians who thought differently about God and the Bible than I did. Later, when I started non-profit work in downtown Nashville, I encountered people from different socioeconomic backgrounds and we became intimately involved in one another's lives. Our organization partnered with all kinds of churches—various denominations that had previously been unfamiliar or even suspect to me. Community was no longer effortless.

For the first time in my life, I felt adrift in the world, unsure of my relational anchors, unsure of where to start. What is it, really, that binds us to another person or to a group of people? "How good and pleasant it is when God's people live together in unity," Psalm 133:1 tells us. But I soon began to realize that I, like many Christians, had experienced unity as uniformity. When it came time for me to learn how to operate outside that uniformity, I was lost.

In Luke chapter 10, Jesus tells a simple story that would go on to become one of his most beloved and oft-cited parables. It is the story of the good Samaritan, and for centuries Christians have taught the anecdote to Sunday school children as an example of how to sacrificially serve those in need. The tale tells of a man beaten by robbers and left for dead on the side of the road, the passersby who couldn't be bothered by his plight, and a caring soul—the Samaritan—who took it upon himself to show mercy and tend to the man's every need.

We often expound upon the various ways the Samaritan provided for this down-on-his-luck traveler—the medical care, the transportation to safety, the shelter—and seek to apply those lessons to our ministries and outreaches. We glean from his good deeds our own strategies for service. We forget, though, to pay attention to the conversation that led to Jesus' telling of the story. It was my friend Dan, a lifelong aid worker, who first pointed out to me that the question posed to Jesus was not *"What should I do* for my neighbor?" but rather *"Who* is my neighbor?" (Luke 10:29). Luke tells us that the person who asked the question, a Jewish expert in the law, was really only trying to justify himself, to validate his prejudice.[1]

Disgust for Samaritans was a common sentiment among many Jewish people of Jesus' day. Seven hundred years earlier, Assyria had invaded the Northern Kingdom of Israel, deporting many of its prominent citizens and resettling the area with foreigners. These pagan Gentiles intermarried with the Jews that remained. Later, when the exiles of the Southern Kingdom returned home after their own captivity in Babylon, they hated the descendants—the Samaritans—of those interracial, interreligious unions.[2] Samaritans had their own versions of the Pentateuch and believed that the epicenter of worship was not the temple in Jerusalem, but rather their temple on Mount Gerizim. Because of this, many Jews saw the Samaritans as worse than Gentiles; they were heretics, maligners of truth, and apostates with unacceptable theology.[3] To hear Jesus say that the Samaritan was the neighbor—that he had been the one to act righteously—would have been repulsive.

But Jesus' answer was part of a larger message he was seeking to communicate with his life and ministry: The gospel is for *all* people. No social, religious, or ethnic group has exclusive access to God, and we should be concerned for the welfare of all God's children, not simply the ones we see as allies.

The question "Who is my neighbor?"—born of a desire to rationalize partiality and ideological egotism—is one we continue to wrestle with today. Even if our prejudices are more subtle, we still want to be around people who are like us. We want our relational lives to be as uncomplicated and painless as possible. Without realizing it, we make mental notes on who is in and who is out, drawing up guidelines to regulate where we invest our energy, who we learn from, and who we pass our time with. We want the comfort of knowing we belong, our friends are close, and our adversaries are kept at a safe distance. Like animals are drawn to the protection of a herd, colony, or flock, it's a primal instinct that draws us to the security of a pack and the solidarity of a shared enemy.

Perhaps underneath the question "Who is my neighbor?" is the more revealing inquiry: "Who, exactly, am I *required* to love?"

And what will that love require of me?

What is it that makes a group of people a community? Is it simply geographic proximity, lines on a map that tell us we vote in the same district, share a zip code, or are zoned to the same school? Is my neighbor really my neighbor if I only know their first name and occasionally wave at them awkwardly from across my lawn? Is community a group of coworkers, fellow members of a church, or a list of followers on social media? And what about those people I don't get along with, my own modern equivalent of a Samaritan? Must I think of *them* as my neighbors? Can I really *commune* with people who have vastly different worldviews than me?

These questions are becoming more and more complicated. Now more than any time in history we have the ability to *choose* our physical neighbors, to carefully select who we keep close. Not only do we have the unprecedented privilege of selecting our marriage partners, but increased mobility allows many of us to move to cities we like, choose school districts we approve of, and live in neighborhoods that make us feel at home. The rise of wage labor means individuals have become more economically independent and no longer need to rely on extended family and kinfolk networks that were so necessary in the past. We retreat to comfortable, hand-picked friend groups. Vehicles enable us to drive to churches that match our theological and programmatic tastes. Air-conditioning shuts us up in our four-bedroom, two-bathroom houses with our nuclear families. Porches are built for privacy, constructed at the back of the home rather than the front where they can be accessed by people from the outside.

We live in a world where much of our human interaction takes place on social media platforms. Algorithms designed to highlight fear and platform rage drive our understanding of one another. We get locked into online echo chambers that validate our opinions and justify our biases.

Social media provide us with the illusion of community yet give us all the control. When we encounter differences of perspective, we can swipe away with a swift movement of the finger. Smartphones serve as the mediator between us and our enemies. Judging and snubbing are done at a safe distance. We can eviscerate someone's character and then log off for the night. We can follow and unfollow, friend and unfriend, mute or block, all without the awkward face-to-face conversation. We can construct a relational life with no skin in the game.

The great myth of social media is that the globalization of our interpersonal connectivity will somehow make us more empathetic, more conscientious, and more relationally whole. We millennials and Gen Zers in particular pride ourselves on our

awareness and on being informed. The entire world is our neighborhood now. The stream of news and media from across the
world surges unceasingly at us via our televisions and phones. We
are expected to post our own geopolitical hot takes when wars
commence and atrocities are committed. We proclaim our rage
when injustices unfold.

But it's hard to know if all this awareness is altruism or voy-
eurism, benevolence or virtue signaling. Sometimes it feels like
we are all cyber rubberneckers, gawking at the suffering of others like drivers on a highway where there's been an accident. We
have a way of nurturing our most unholy curiosities, of consuming
the pain of others without being willing to do the hard work of
meaningfully addressing the problem. We believe that we are part
of a global community. But in many ways, our relational lives are
smaller and more self-centric than ever before.

When I think of building community, my first instinct is
to surround myself with like-minded friends who see the world
exactly the same way I do, who will see *me* in the way I want to
be seen. These are the people I "do life" with, the friends I know
will always have my back and be in my corner. We were drawn to
one another through common interests, because of shared likes
and dislikes. Call them "besties," or a "tribe," or a "squad." We
validate one another, have fun together, get mad about the same
things, and make each other feel at home in the world. These
are the people who will make me happy, or so I assume.

The history of the word "community" reveals that our ancestors
may have thought differently about their relational ties. The Latin
communitas is derived from the more ancient Indo-European terms
kom (meaning "with" or "next to") and *munus* (meaning "employment," "service," "duty," or "obligation").[4] While our culture tends

to emphasize shared ideas as the glue that holds people together, societies in the past likely saw shared *labor* as the deeper binding agent of a community. Communal life was formed by of the neighbors who plowed fields together, villagers who bought and sold goods from one another, and the extended family and household members who labored together under the same roof. They needed one another not just for affirmation but for survival.

Get connected. Plug in. Share life. Go deeper.

Christians are indeed promised great gains if they can effectively build community. We look back on the early Church of Acts—how they broke bread together and shared everything in common—with longing and nostalgia. The communal life of these ancient believers was marked by sacrifice, study of the Word, the sharing of meals, and service to those most in need. Churches today still value these practices, claiming that they are foundational to who we are. Christians often speak of simplifying, of trying to "keep the main thing the main thing." But the way we spend our time and money often reveals different values.

In a consumer culture that invites us to "have it your way," the church of today sometimes looks more like a business venture, or, as pastor and author Skye Jethani says, an "industrial complex."[5] Beyond the megachurches—whose average budget is $5.3 million[6]—a growing network of parachurch organizations, Christian media companies, Christian record labels, and Christian publishers, now exist to feed the faith-based consumer market. By the time I was growing up evangelical in the '80s and '90s, the Christian subculture had grown into a massive commercial enterprise, complete with its own celebrities, movies, music, bookstores, and even theme parks.

I understand that in a world where so much is vying for our attention, Christians feel the pressure to keep up. As early as 1853, Charles Finney, the fiery Presbyterian revivalist who helped initiate the Second Great Awakening, wrote:

> Without new measures it is impossible that the church should succeed in gaining the attention of the world to religion. There are so many exciting subjects constantly brought before the public mind, such a running to and fro, so many that cry "Lo here," and "Lo there," that the church cannot maintain her ground, cannot command attention, without very exciting preaching, and sufficient novelty in measures, to get the public ear.[7]

Finney fought hard to maintain that ground. According to historian Jeanne Halgren Kilde, author of the book *When Church Became Theatre*, we owe the architectural design of most of our modern churches to him. In the 1830s, Finney rented one of the largest theaters in New York City and outfitted it to house his growing church, the Free Presbyterian Chatham Street Chapel. So successful were his rousing revivals and church services that other congregations began to follow suit, designing their churches with sloped auditorium-style seating and large stages. The spatial design of these sanctuaries offered a great advantage to church leaders who, like Finney, were increasingly structuring their services around two key elements: a lively sermon and a rapturous musical presentation.[8]

I've heard it said that the architecture of a church acts as a kind of spiritual formation. There's something about meeting as a community of faith in a theater that encourages spectatorship over participation, consumption over service. When you spend an hour and a half staring at a stage rather than an altar, everything about a Sunday morning takes on an undertone of entertainment, of performance. It's easy for church to become a place where we gather to consume content, rather than to commune in love. Too often, what binds us together is not our shared passion for Christ, but rather our shared preference for a particular product.

If a church's architecture is spiritual formation, then so is its address. The early to mid-twentieth century was a time when white middle-class Americans began to flee the pollution, congestion, and noise of city centers and move to the suburbs. Many were also fleeing the desegregation in urban areas brought on by the civil rights movement. White churches were faced with a dilemma: Should they remain downtown where economic and social needs were often the greatest? Or should they also withdraw to the outskirts of the city to better accommodate the desires of their wealthiest attendees?[9] Church was becoming a competitive business by then. Big theaters, plus professional musicians, plus hotshot preachers caught the eyes of potential members, but they also came with price tags.

By and large, the suburbs won the day.

The address and architecture of a church are indeed spiritual formation. When you are surrounded every Sunday by a bunch of white, middle-class suburbanites, you can be led to subconsciously believe that Christianity is inherently white and affluent, to think of Jesus himself as white and affluent. Though it was never spoken of in the churches I grew up in, a close look at history reveals that many white churches have often been complicit in the injustices imposed on people of color. In some cases, it was white church leaders themselves who were helping to orchestrate the injustice. Writes author and historian Jemar Tisby: "Historically speaking, when faced with the choice between racism and equality, the American church has tended to practice a complicit Christianity rather than a courageous Christianity. They chose comfort over constructive conflict and in so doing created and maintained a status quo of injustice."[10]

Like the religious elites of Jesus' day who despised the Samaritans, our love is sadly sometimes overtaken by fear—fear of "the other," fear of discomfort, fear of losing control and influence. In the decades that followed the church's retreat to the suburbs, white evangelicals, galvanized by a few key political issues, coalesced to become one of America's most powerful voting blocs. By the time I was of voting age, white evangelicals were being persistently courted by political candidates, and entire media news outlets existed to cater to their viewing desires.

This civic clout has not always been used in ways that are consistent with biblical values. While immigrants of faith arriving in America have proven to be a beacon of hope in an otherwise bleak and declining religious landscape, white evangelicals are unfortunately one of the most anti-immigrant demographics and political groups in this nation.[11] In 1960, Martin Luther King Jr. famously observed that "eleven o'clock on Sunday morning is one of the most segregated hours, if not *the* most segregated hour, in Christian America."[12] These words, spoken more than sixty years ago, sadly remain largely true.

Yes, we want to "share life" together. But we have a hard time sharing it with people who are different from us, who make us uncomfortable, whose testimonies and circumstances challenge us to give up something we hold dear. And I understand the feeling. Looking back, I realize that one of the things I valued most about my community was how little it required of me. I could actually "have it my way." Skye Jethani, in his book *The Divine Commodity*, admits to what so many of us struggle with when it comes to our expectations of Christian community:

> I want my desires fulfilled and pain minimized. I want a manageable relationship with an institution rather than messy relationships with real people. I want to be transformed into the image of Christ by showing up at entertaining events rather than through the hard work of discipleship…And above all, I want a controllable god. I want a divine commodity to do my will on earth as well as in heaven.[13]

My fear is that the nature of the Christian subculture has conditioned Jesus followers like me to believe one of the most subtle and insidious lies of the emotional prosperity gospel: the tacit belief that Christianity is above all safe, entertaining, and comfortable. It is the perception of Christian community as politically advantageous, socially beneficial, and personally profitable. The complicated truth is that Christianity has made some people very, very wealthy and very, very powerful. And that wealth and power are often seen as assets rather than liabilities.

Author and cultural critic Neil Postman writes, "I believe and I am not mistaken in saying that Christianity is a demanding and serious religion. When it is delivered as easy and amusing, it is another kind of religion altogether."[14]

Ce~

I'm certainly not the first person to observe that the relational lives of many Americans seem to be faltering. Communication technology is innovating at such a high rate of speed that sometimes it feels like our ethics and emotional coping mechanisms haven't caught up. We are busy and overwhelmed by an oversupply of connections, but only a few of those connections seem to be meeting our deepest need for belonging. In a survey conducted just before the pandemic, three out of five Americans reported feeling lonely.[15] Our relational lives sometimes seem to be a thousand miles wide and an inch deep.

We are not the first generation to worry that changes in technology and economics would irrevocably harm our social lives. In 2023, we decry social media as the culprit. In the late 1800s, it was the telephone and telegraph. These speedy correspondence devices, plus urbanization, mobilization, and growing consumerism, made the late Victorians fear that the conventional morals and old social networks of traditional, small-town communities would permanently break down.[16]

In response to this moral panic, leaders got busy forming social organizations. Veteran, religious, fraternal, labor, and civic groups exploded. The Red Cross, NAACP, Audubon Society, Boy Scouts, Girl Scouts, Goodwill, Kiwanis, and American Legion were all established in the late nineteenth and early twentieth centuries. Basically, we became a nation of clubs.[17]

In his groundbreaking book *Bowling Alone: The Collapse and Revival of American Community*, Robert D. Putnam observes that there are two forms of social capital: bonding and bridging. Some organizations are *bonding* by nature, meaning that they attract people of the same social, ethnic, or economic group. These associations are inward facing and tend to reinforce their members' existing ideas and opinions. But many of the organizations formed at the turn of the century were *bridging* organizations by nature. Bridging associations draw together people from different backgrounds and perspectives. They provide exposure to new ideas and dismantle stereotypes. Writes Putnam, "Bonding social capital constitutes a kind of sociological superglue, whereas bridging social capital provides a sociological WD-40."[18] Bridging organizations might be more emotionally and relationally challenging, but in the end, they help a diverse society function with empathy and openhandedness.

Unfortunately, participation in these civic organizations and social clubs is in significant decline across America. Involvement in everything from parent-teacher associations to Rotary Clubs, and veterans' organizations to labor unions is decreasing.[19] As many businesses move to a "work from home" model, we are losing even the relational touchpoint of the workplace.

It seems to me that we are constructing our lives around only bonding organizations and bonding mechanisms: algorithmically curated social media echo chambers, the nuclear family, homogenized churches, and small, carefully selected friend groups. Office spaces shared by people of various demographics and political persuasions are disappearing. Perhaps what we really need are more *bridging* opportunities. We need to be in proximity to people who challenge our thinking, expose us to new viewpoints, and disrupt stereotypes with their physical presence.

In a culture facing an epidemic of loneliness, more and more studies show that there is at least one activity that is almost always guaranteed to mitigate that loneliness: volunteerism. One recent study, for example, measured the feelings of aloneness among widows. While the death of a spouse was shown to significantly increase levels of loneliness, widows who volunteered two or more hours a week showed the same level of loneliness as their married peers.[20] In other words, regular volunteerism proved to alleviate loneliness significantly.

I suppose being reminded that you can live as a contributor and not merely as a consumer is deeply encouraging. We humanize ourselves when we volunteer. And we humanize others. Volunteering forces you to rub shoulders with people who are different from you, be it the beneficiaries of your service or your co-volunteers. Perhaps the most invigorating aspect of volunteerism is the powerful connection that is formed by a shared mission. A common goal takes our eyes off the petty differences that divide us. It lifts our eyes to something that is good and true, to our shared needs and mutual humanity.

I think the thing that saved me when I felt communally adrift was my work in social services and in humanitarian aid. When you join a group of people who are working hard at providing housing, food, and water to people in crisis, you don't have a whole lot of time to tarry over personality differences or even ideological disagreements. The work requires you to stand arm in arm with people who voted differently, who are from different parts of the world, and who hold to different theological positions. But we are united around a common cause and a core shared belief that Jesus called us to love our neighbors in need. While there is a part of me that longs for the ease of uniformity, the unity I've found over a shared labor of love has been a deeper, richer form of blessing than I've ever known.

If ever there was an entity that should be united around a shared mission, it is the Church. It is the heaviness and beauty of that mission—not the programs or the products or political power—that should serve as the unbreakable bonding agent. The challenge for the Church is to do all we can to make our congregations both bonding *and* bridging. We bond—of course—over our shared love for Christ, but we cannot stop there. We must bridge the divides that exist between us and outsiders, between us and other Christians who don't look or think exactly like we do.

While the psalmist describes Christian community as "good" and "pleasant" (Ps. 133:1), the writer of Proverbs gives us a less appealing depiction of godly friendship: "As iron sharpens iron, so one person sharpens another" (27:17). Metal on metal is not always comfortable. But it is a holy discomfort. It's hard to imagine how a person of faith can ever grow spiritually if their ideas are never challenged, if new perspectives are never presented. How can we grow in our understanding and compassion when we refuse to expose ourselves to people who are different from us? How can we learn to love more deeply when we are not given the chance to love those who are hard for us to love? How can we be discipled to lay down our lives when our pastors are just like pundits who tell us political power is all that matters? As Postman observed, Christianity is indeed demanding and serious. But how can we train our souls to rise to that demand when we've constructed a "religion" that demands nothing of us?

Ce ~

It's hard to guess what would shock the early Church fathers and mothers most if they were to live one day in the shoes of a modern

American Christian. The immeasurable sway that evangelicals have in the market and in politics would likely astonish them. The massive amount of resources allocated for marketing and entertainment would probably be equally appalling. They no doubt would be grieved by the divide that continues to persist between believers of different racial and socioeconomic groups.

The early Church—who, according to Acts, shared everything in common—didn't have a marketing strategy. They "won" converts by the power of their simple witness and quality of their communal love. They made a name for themselves by their radical sacrifice on behalf of the poor and abandoned. It was a *true* community made up of people from all kinds of backgrounds, bloodlines, and income levels.

The early Church met not at a time and place that was advantageous to courting the wealthy and powerful. Instead, they met during the predawn hours of Sunday morning because that was the only time that slaves and women—a valued demographic of the Church—could feasibly escape their household responsibilities and the watchful eye of their masters.[21] They didn't meet in theaters. In fact, because the Church of the first and second centuries was not recognized by the Roman government, it could not own property. So, Christians met in homes. Or catacombs.[22] It was not exactly a "seeker-sensitive" model by today's standards. It was not even close to the "church experience" so many of us strive to create in our modern-day congregations. To follow Christ was not politically or financially advantageous. It was not safe by any stretch of the imagination.

There is a feeling of security that comes with a custom-made Christian subculture. But there is a very real and present danger in believing that the preservation of that subculture is what God meant when he told us to dwell together in love and unity. I do not begrudge my experience growing up in that subculture. It was, in many ways, a blessing to me. But whether by design or by default, it was only a partial picture of true community. The blessing was incomplete.

Tim likes to say that there are some blessings—like marriage and parenthood and community—that are inherently emotionally costly. He says that if these blessings cost you nothing, you are doing something wrong. A small group or church community filled with people who look exactly like me, think exactly like me, and only ever make me feel good about myself may *feel* like happiness. But it is a thin and counterfeit form of true happiness.

Real community is indeed demanding and serious. The Christian life is demanding and serious. So often in life, we want the good thing without those necessary costs that come with it. We want the joys of parenthood without the tasks. We want decadent food without heartburn. We want a clean environment without having to give up our gas-guzzling SUVs. We want the elimination of poverty without having to sacrifice our own affluence. We want the benefits of community without the demands or duties of it. We like the idea of diversity, but we don't want the effort of diversifying to inconvenience our actual lives.

But loving others well is inherently inconvenient. Community, by its very nature, is perilous to the ego. When you truly invest in a relationship, you risk being hurt. When you love your neighbor, not just your clique, you risk being challenged. You risk being exposed or told you might be wrong. You risk being asked to give more than you get, to experience as many withdrawals as deposits.

The muscle memory of consumerism is entitlement, the expectation of immediate gratification, and a wariness of too much expenditure. The slow and difficult work of building community dethrones the customer. It calls us to sow seeds that may never turn into a harvest. It invites us to stay—at least sometimes—when all we want to do is run. I'm learning that in losing yourself, sometimes you find yourself in new ways. As physician and author Richard Swenson writes, "Love is the only medicine I know of which, when used according to directions, heals completely yet takes one's life away. It is dangerous; it is uncontrollable; it is 'self-expenditure'; and it can never be taken on any terms but its own. Yet as a healer of the emotions, it has no equal."[23]

No doubt, there *are* people who have readily opened their hearts to racial and socioeconomic diversity. Many are eager to swing wide the doors for cross-cultural engagement. But no matter how open and welcoming any of us may be, there will always be *that* person, the one you could never imagine "going deeper" with or "doing life" with. Sometimes, what Jesus is asking of us is to lay down our enmity and build a bridge to the person we find the most difficult, most suspicious, most unlike us—whoever that may be. Draw near to them, not necessarily to adopt all their beliefs as our own, but in curiosity, to simply learn more. This will require humility, an authentic willingness to admit the limitations of our own perspective. But survival in this increasingly polarized world depends on our ability to build bridges.

My friend Dan, who shed new light for me on the story of the good Samaritan, has certainly had his perspective shaped by years of global humanitarian work. Dan understood what Jesus was trying to communicate, that the question "Who is my neighbor?" is too often asked in arrogance, assuming that *I*, and people like me, are the only ones who really have something to offer the world. At its core, the story is not about the specifics of rendering aid to someone, but is rather a revelation that goodness often resides in the people and places we least expect. Jesus was asking his listeners to do the unthinkable: Emulate a Samaritan. Do we allow ourselves to be shaped by the people we may have some misgivings about? Are we willing to admit that we actually *need* people who are different from us?

The emotional prosperity gospel calls us to the security of tribes and squads, tells us there is safety in numbers of like-minded people and blessing to be found in sameness and similarities. But Jesus tells us to go beyond the walls of our ideological fortresses and theological temples. Like he told the Samaritan woman at the well, there will come a day when we won't worship at the temple of Jerusalem or the temple on Gerizim. Rather, we will simply worship in Spirit and truth with the true worshippers—"for they are the kind of worshipers the Father seeks" (John 4:23). Community is indeed key to a happy life. But the greatest blessings of community can only be found when we are willing to see and to seek out all people as the Father sees and seeks.

It was the socially acceptable and religiously safe characters who ended up passing by the poor man in the ditch in Jesus' story—a priest and a Levite. Instead, it was the Samaritan—the outcast who chafed against the listeners' social and religious sensibilities—who said yes to the call to serve. Jesus concludes the story with his own question: "Which of these three do you think was a neighbor to the man who fell into the hands of robbers?" (Luke 10:36). The expert in the law couldn't even allow the detestable word "Samaritan" to escape from his lips. He simply replied, "The one who had mercy on him" (v. 37).

Jesus ends with this simple charge: "Go and do likewise" (v. 37).

CHAPTER 6

BODY

(Serve with All Your Strength)

In the summer of 2002, I was eighteen years old and two months away from going off to college. I was excited. My bedroom was piled high with suitcases stuffed with new clothes and boxes packed with sentimental trinkets, family photos, and poetry books. I was enrolled at a Christian liberal arts school just thirty miles north of New York City. This small-town, East Tennessee girl was ready to spread her wings and fly, ready to see the big, wide world.

But then, one afternoon, I developed an ache in my stomach. That ache, over the course of just a few hours, intensified into body-shaking cramps. Searing waves of pain shot through my abdomen and around my back. Around midnight, the bleeding started, and my parents rushed me to the hospital.

I don't remember much from my time at the hospital, only that I was delirious from the pain and weak from dehydration. Doctors urgently ordered blood work, scans, and scopes. These tests revealed the source of my sickness. My colon had become spontaneously inflamed. The walls of my digestive organs looked like they'd been sliced up with a razor blade. In the words of my nurse, "I've never seen angrier intestines in my entire life."

It was the medical emergency I never saw coming. I'd been perfectly healthy, working outside as a groundskeeper every day, hiking with my friends, serving at church, and packing and prepping for my new life at school. I was immediately given a high dose of steroids, painkillers, and anti-inflammatories. Various consultants and specialists came to my room to examine me. One of my only memories from the hospital is waking up from anesthesia after a test, throwing my arms around my father, and telling him, "Dad, I'm scared."

Eventually the bleeding stopped, and the pain subsided enough for me to be sent home. I left the hospital with bags of pills and no clear diagnosis. Crohn's disease perhaps, or severe ulcerative colitis? The doctor told my parents, "Your daughter will likely be sick the rest of her life."

The weight of that statement never really sank in. Those first few days home from the hospital, I was living hour to hour, coming off the haze of painkillers, learning my new meds schedule, and eating dry toast to try to regain my strength. My parents attempted to encourage me, but I saw in their eyes that grave look of worry and fear for my future. Would I be able to go to college? Would I be spending my life in bed, in and out of hospitals? How long could I survive with this mysterious disease?

My dad did the only thing he knew to do. Every night, after I'd drifted off to sleep, he'd come into my room, kneel by my bed, and pray for a miracle. He asked God to heal me.

And, as fate—or Providence, I suppose—would have it, God did heal me.

This was not a slow, progressive miracle. It was not realized gradually over time as health and vitality eventually set in. It was not achieved by some pharmaceutical feat or miracle diet. I did not juice or cleanse or cut out meat or sugar. I just got better. Almost immediately. By day four, I was up and about, helping my mom with dishes and spending time with friends who'd come to visit. A week after coming home from the hospital, I had no pain, no bleeding, no problem eating or drinking. My energy returned, I put on the weight I'd lost, and—to my great relief—I was able to finish packing my bags for college. It was as if nothing had ever happened. It was like I was given a second chance at life.

For years after that, I met with doctors and specialists, seeking answers for what had occurred that summer. My body was monitored, my blood was drawn, annual tests performed to make sure the inflammation had not returned. Every scan came back clear; every scope indicated perfect health. And every doctor I've met since that summer has reached the same conclusion: They have no idea what happened to me. They have no clue how I became sick so suddenly and well so quickly. I am a living, breathing medical mystery. I am a walking miracle.

I'd ventured close to death, had peered over the edge into the void of an untimely end, or—at the very least—a life of physical suffering. But God had answered the prayers of my faithful father. I'd come out victorious and newly strengthened. I'd come home healed. God was good and I was happy.

Most of us come into life with a long list of demands for our bodies, or at least a long list of dreams. We want to be healthy and strong, and it certainly wouldn't hurt to be beautiful. "Love the

Lᴏʀᴅ your God with all your heart and with all your soul and with all your strength," the children of Israel are told in Deuteronomy 6:5 as God begins to outline the decrees and commands. I figured if God wanted me to serve him with my body, then he would provide for me a body that was strong, willing, and able. This belief was only reinforced by the fact that I entered adulthood with all the euphoria of a health crisis averted. My medical miracle was like a feather in my cap.

This is not to say that I believed my body would never be susceptible to suffering. As a passionate critic of the prosperity gospel, I knew that pain could not always be prayed away, and that illness and death could not always be overcome by the power of a positive mindset. If Christians were indeed called to "offer [their] bodies as a living sacrifice" (Rom. 12:1), then physical risk was part of the deal. *I could die here*, I'd think to myself every time I deplaned in a war zone or disaster zone. I could get malaria, our car could hit an IED, or I could be kidnapped. I was mentally and emotionally prepared to suffer for Jesus in this way. I was taking calculated risks, setting my safety aside for the sake of a cause I cared about.

The way I saw it, God had work for me to do in the world, and so I always thought that work would be *helped* by my body, and never *hindered* by it. "I can do all things through Christ who strengthens me" (Phil. 4:13 ɴᴋᴊᴠ), I'd repeat to myself over and over again when faced with a challenge. This much-beloved—and much-misunderstood—verse gave me a sense of limitlessness. I thought my body would carry me to my calling, that these muscles and bones would build the kingdom brick by brick. I had a mission. I had blood, sweat, and tears to shed. I was willing and eager. I thought I could "run and not grow weary" (Isa. 40:31), as if good intentions were the ultimate performance-enhancing drug.

As life rolled forward and I continued to engage my body in service for the Lord in those war zones, disaster zones, and in church and family life—which can sometimes feel like a disaster zone—I never stopped to count the toll that the labor had taken on my body. I thought I could bypass the physical implications of stress, grief, and even injury—like I could outsmart the costs of life's hardships. "Thank you very much, Dr. Van der Kolk, but *my* body does *not* keep the score." What doesn't kill *me* makes me stronger. I will stand in defiance over my body and direct it, demand that it improve. I can *will* it to be well.

Most Westerners carry with them a subtle but pervasive dualism handed down by ancient Greek philosophers like Plato and Aristotle. We operate as if the mind and the body are separate. My mind is the storehouse of my soul, the place where my thoughts and judgments arise. My body, on the other hand, is the keeper of my fleshly desires and passions.[1] The superior of the two is the mind, and I like to think it can make my body do whatever I want it to do. By sheer force of desire, I can muscle through whatever life throws my way. Mind over matter, emotional strength over physical weakness. Like the New Thought mesmerist, I believed in the power of positive thinking to coerce my body into submission.

I made the mistake of assuming that because God had obviously wanted my eighteen-year-old body to be well, that he'd want my thirty-year-old body to be well and eventually my forty-year-old body to be well also. But in the last year or two, I have been plagued by health challenges that have my doctors scratching their heads. A shoulder injury I acquired while rocking my daughter during her first weeks of life hasn't gotten better, despite rest and physical therapy. A bruise on my knee has led to a persistent pain in my leg. An internal organ started inexplicably failing. (Fortunately, it was a nonessential organ—the gallbladder.) Nevertheless, these pains have kept me up most nights for the better part of a year, leaving me wondering if I'll feel anything but tired ever again.

Mentally and spiritually, I am ready to serve. How could I let something as banal as the body keep me from living the life God clearly wanted me to live? For years, I took my physical vigor for granted, assumed my flesh would always work in my favor if I willed it to do so. I never thought something as drab and unsexy as "angry intestines," a nonfunctional gallbladder, or bursitis in the shoulder would curtail my best-laid plans.

If my body was the temple of the Lord, then why was I having to take time off from leading worship at church because of a shoulder injury that simply wasn't getting better? If my body was designed for motherhood, then why had I struggled so much to conceive and maintain a pregnancy? Why do I continue to struggle so much to recover from birthing and breastfeeding my daughters? If I was to serve the Lord with all my strength, then what was I to do if my strength started to fail? If I'd made all the right decisions about my health—said no to drugs, eaten a balanced diet, exercised three to four times a week—then why was I not experiencing wellness? There was so much I wanted to do, so much I *needed* to do. I can't describe to you the level of shock I felt when I suddenly realized I *could not*. I had reached my limit. I could not be everything I wanted to be. My body would not let me.

It is amazing how much we know about the human body. We've come a long way since the days of medical antiquity, since theories about wandering uteruses and imbalanced humours. Imagine living in a world without germ theory or molecular biology. The practice of medicine was all but a guessing game in generations past. But now we have technologies like MRI machines and CAT scanners that allow us to study bodily organs in exquisite detail. Blood tests allow doctors to do a biochemical analysis of a patient with a simple prick of a needle in the arm. We have unprecedented knowledge about pulmonology, immunology, neurobiology, and endocrinology. Scientists can engineer lifesaving drugs and doctors can perform laparoscopic, laser, and robotic surgeries with meticulous precision. All of this has led to rising life expectancy and a higher quality of life for people around the globe.

This deluge of knowledge and medical advancements can create a feeling of invincibility and bodily omniscience. If there is a problem, we assume we can ascertain the cause and apply a lifesaving solution. We live and operate as if we are immortal. But the hard reality is, there is so much about the human body we still don't fully understand, so much we can't control. Doctors don't know why some people experience pain more acutely than others. Scientists can't explain from an evolutionary perspective why we have unique fingerprints and different blood types. New viruses emerge, attacking the body in such perplexing and innovative ways that the medical world can't outsmart them. The mystery of human consciousness is perhaps the greatest enigma of all. What is it in my brain, exactly, that gives me this internal, enduring sense of identity, awareness, and existence?

The mystery of the body and limits of medical science are a tough pill to swallow for the most informed generation the world has ever known. The boundaries of medical intervention became painfully real to me four years ago when my sister, Rachel, died suddenly after battling a strange and sudden illness. She'd come down with a bad bout of the flu, but then she unexpectedly began experiencing static brain seizures that no combination of medication and treatment could stop. Neurological experts from around the country considered her case and no one could precisely explain why the seizures had started or what might stop them.

My dad did the same thing for her that he had done for me. He knelt by her bed every day and prayed for a miracle, asked God to intervene. But after almost three weeks of being sick, her brain started swelling, and she died.

I live my life squeezed between these two medical mysteries— my sudden illness and hers, my positive outcome and her deadly one. Why does God say yes when he does? Why does he say no? Why did I get to live, and why did she have to die? I feel the pressing of these two realities against my soul, against my body, every single day.

I used to take great comfort in statistics. If a well-researched scientist told me that I had a pretty decent shot at living, I didn't waste my emotional energy believing anything different. Up until my mid-thirties, the statistics had always been on my side. I was a young, middle-class, privileged woman. Secure housing. Secure domestic relationships. Secure neighborhood. I had access to leafy greens, and I ate them regularly. All my grandparents had lived to a ripe old age. I'd even miraculously survived an episode of exploding intestines. Data doesn't lie, I'd tell myself. I've got as good a chance as anyone at having a long, healthy life. And so do the people I love.

After my first miscarriage, I reassured myself by reading all the statistics about how unlikely it was for me to have a second miscarriage. When my sister was first hospitalized with the flu, I pored over survival rates, which were astronomically high for someone her age.

But then, I had another miscarriage. Then another. And my sister died.

Statistics are indeed comforting. Unless *you* are the 1 percent. Or the 0.01 percent. Then you feel betrayed by science, hoodwinked by the universe. "It's not supposed to be this way," you scream at the data, and your whole life becomes a variation on that theme. You turn out to be the anomaly, the exception to the rule. There is nothing I hate more than a medical mystery. Especially when the mystery is an unhappy one.

After Rachel's death, I met with my ICU nurse practitioner friend who happened to be working at the hospital where my sister was being treated. She was there with Rachel when she died. I asked her if she could shed any light on the reason for my sister's death. She told me that sometimes, catastrophic medical events occur without much explanation. Unexplained deaths still happen frequently, she said, more than the medical community likes to admit.

And isn't it so true—none of us want to admit how vulnerable we are, how limited we are, how precarious our lives can be. Our privilege, prosperity, and reassuring statistics about long life expectancy have given us the illusion of control, the feeling of indomitability.

As the saying goes—we don't even know what we don't know. We are all teetering on the edge of the unknown unknowns.

The embodied myth of the emotional prosperity gospel is that if we *want* to do a good thing for God, then we will absolutely be able to do it. God will give us the physical and spiritual stamina to do it. We hold in our minds an ideal image of what service looks like, what strength entails, and what heights are possible.

Whether or not I care to admit it, I've always desired a body that measured up to this internalized ideal. Sadly, this ideal has been shaped in many ways by toxic cultural forces as well as derogatory attitudes within religious circles. It wasn't just strength I wanted—it was bodily perfection. Societal standards or norms regarding beauty, goodness, desirability, health, and capacity have informed how we judge the bodies of others and judge our own bodies. Over the years, racism, ageism, and ableism—all prejudices that denigrate human bodies—have pervaded the Church just as they have culture at large.[2]

Scholar and disability advocate Amy Kenny is a woman who has experienced the harmful impact of these internalized ideals. Reflecting on what it is like to have everyone around her believe that her body needs fixing, she writes:

> To assume that my disability needs to be erased in order for me to live an abundant life is disturbing not only because of what it says about me but also because of what it reveals about people's notions of God. I bear the image of the Alpha and Omega. My disabled body is a temple for the Holy Spirit…To suggest that I am anything less than sanctified and redeemed is to suppress the image of God in my disabled body and to limit how God is already at work through my life.[3]

Christians have not always lived up to their anthropological ethic. We have not honored the image-bearing bodies God has given us. The Church has repeatedly shown its cards, whether by insisting that disabled or ailing bodies must be cured in order for God to be good, or by publishing a slew of Christian diet books beginning in the 1960s—books with appalling titles like *I Prayed Myself Slim* (1960); *Jesus Wants You Well* (1973); *"Help Lord—The Devil Wants Me Fat!"* (1982); *What Would Jesus Eat?* (2002); and *Thin Within* (2005). We associate goodness with health, with productivity, and with the world's definition of beauty. One only has to witness the vast number of "beach body" selfies on social media posted with the hashtag #blessed to recognize how shallow our understanding of blessing is.

Growing up, I noticed the people who were given platforms, not just in the secular media but also in the Church. I saw the types of bodies who made it to the stages of ministry. So often, they fit a particular mold, had a marketable quality to their appearance that I desired for myself. Something in me felt like I'd be missing out on God's best for me if my body didn't meet these impossible and unjust standards. If my life was supposed to be like some exciting epic adventure, like a script that was movie-worthy, it simply wouldn't do for the heroine (me) to be anything less than healthy, energetic, and beautiful.

So, I pushed my body. Hard. I punished it. I spent much of my teens and twenties on and off fad diets. I had no concept of healthy eating; only eating to lose weight, to drop a dress size, to fit into a pair of jeans. There were months when my eating habits edged close to dangerous, with severely reduced calories and grueling exercise regimens. When the cracks started to show, when my body became sick or exhausted, I pushed it even harder, not wanting to acknowledge my limits or admit that I was tired and in pain. Weariness was unacceptable. Rest was for the weak. Hunger could be overcome with grit and resolve.

I had this one shot at life, this one chance to be in the world, to serve, and to achieve. My soul needed a vehicle to carry it to all the heights I hoped for. If my body was a temple of the Lord, then I wanted that temple to be beautiful, sturdy, impressive, and built to last. I was all in on this particular myth of the blessed life: Dedicate yourself to God's service, and your strength will be limitless. Pour yourself out like a drink offering, and your cup will never run dry.

When I look back on that time of frenzied dieting and staunch resistance to fragility, I see a person who didn't know how to love her body—who didn't even know how to think about her body. I see someone who had a broken understanding of both beauty and strength. I remember bookmarking Psalm 16 in my Bible, tracing the words of verse 9 over and over again until my fingers nearly wore a hole in the page: "Therefore my heart is glad and my tongue rejoices; my body also will rest secure." How in the world could *my* body—my tired, imperfect, hungry, self-loathing body—rest secure? I was the picture of *in*security. What even was my body to me? Did it have any value at all? Why couldn't I stop thinking about it, worrying about it, striving to perfect it?

Scripture presents Christians with a significant amount of complexity related to our physicality. We live with the reality that our bodies have the capacity to know both pain and pleasure, to commit acts of kindness and harm. We encounter the dissonance that exists between verses that tell us our bodies are temporary, "earthly tent[s]" (2 Cor. 5:1) and verses that tell us they are destined for resurrection (see 1 Cor. 15:42). There are verses that describe our bodies as a living sacrifice (see Rom. 12:1) but others that tell us the carnal desires of our flesh wage war against the Spirit (see Gal. 5:17). We know that we are fearfully and wonderfully made (see Ps. 139:14); and yet our flesh is fleeting, withering like the grass (see 1 Pet. 1:24). Our bodies are temples of the Holy Spirit (see 1 Cor. 6:19); and yet we are but dust (see Ps. 103:14).

Still, the story of creation continually reminds us that there is something inherently good about our physical bodies, something precious even. It is not just my soul that bears God's image; it is also my skin and bones. Creation groans, but it is still good. Our bodies are part of that creation and so they groan as well. No amount of ministerial aspirations or goal-setting for God can alleviate the hazards of living in a body. But our bodies, like creation, are still good. Bodies of all shapes, ethnicities, ages, and abilities breathe the very breath of God. They each exist not as tokens or fodder for inspirational stories, but as functional contributors to the kingdom of God.

Theologian John W. Kleinig refers to the body as a "constant companion." He writes, "It locates me in a particular place at a particular time with particular people in my particular society, family, marriage, and workplace. I am born with my body and die when it can no longer sustain me...I experience the world around me through it. I live with my body and do everything with it. My human life is, most obviously and simply, life in the body."[4] I depend on my body to be in the world. I desperately need it. Why, then, do I begrudge it so?

Like so many things in life, we often reject a body we deem is not perfect. I spent my adolescence hating my body for what I perceived was its unattractiveness. In my thirties, I traded that resentment in for a new one. I now berate my body for its physical limits, deride it for not always doing my bidding. I'm frustrated that it didn't get pregnant on cue, that it struggled to breastfeed my second daughter, that it is too tired to take me to all the places I want to go, that it is sometimes too sick to get out of bed. I'm angry at it for being in pain. I hate that I cannot do all the things I desire to do. I talk down to my body, abuse it, dismiss it.

But unlike a job or a relationship, you can't leave your body just because you don't like it anymore. You can't quit your skin. Wherever I go, my body goes with me. We can put it on a fad diet, can give it supplements and juices. We can drug it, palliate it, treat it. But we can't vacate it, at least not without dying. And since most of us fear death, we stay. And we stay frustrated.

"You should probably rest," I've heard doctors say to me more than once, especially as they've sought to understand my chronic pain. "Slow down a little," they say. But if there is no rest for the weary, then there is certainly no rest for the eager, the earnest, the ambitious. There is no respite from the project of self-actualization. There is no reprieve from the pursuit of happiness.

It has taken me a while, but I am finally beginning to learn that true strength is not the same as limitlessness. Pastor and author Peter Scazzero writes,

Limits offer us many gifts. They protect us so we don't hurt ourselves, others, or God's work. They keep us grounded and humble, reminding us that we are not in charge of running the world. They break our self-will…and they are one of the primary ways we grow in wisdom. And perhaps most importantly, limits are places we encounter God in ways that would otherwise be impossible.[5]

Like most modern Americans, I have a hard time thinking of my limits as a gift. Even as a Christian, who clings to a religion that lists Sabbath rest as one of its top ten most important commandments, I struggle to accept my need for respite. My body is drawn to the drumbeat of productivity and performance-driven ministry. I want to do more for God. I want to *be* more for him.

And, of course, I want to do more for *me*. I want to be more for *me*.

But many days, I feel like a phone on the last 1 percent of battery, like a car running on fumes. I fear I will break down, that I'll experience an all-systems failure, that I'll disappear. In these moments, it seems like life is defrauding me of goodness, like I've been bamboozled out of the blessing. "The sky is the limit," the world convinces us. Time-saving products tempt me to believe I can accomplish endless tasks on any given day. I'm sold supplements that supposedly give my body the energy it needs to go another mile and another. The phone in my pocket can take me to a million places on earth, connect me to a billion people, feed my brain whatever data it desires. I have all the tools, all the information, all the extras, all the connectivity, all the power.

But the sky is not the limit. My *body* is the limit. It is okay to say, "I cannot do that." Or even to say, "I will not do that." Interestingly, when Paul says, "I can do all things through Christ who strengthens me," he is actually talking about learning to be content with less, to be satisfied with constraints. Contrary to what the self-help industry and sports apparel companies would tell us, we cannot always "just do it." The great lie of the wellness movement is that, despite all its claims of rest and self-acceptance, the goal is *still* productivity. The aim is still enhancement. Become a better version of yourself. Rest to be your best. Or, in the words of the Roman poet Ovid, "A field that has rested gives a beautiful crop."[6]

But our bodies cannot sustain the constant optimizations and enhancements and upgrades. No amount of rest will supply the recuperation we need from the world we live in. We were not made to multitask at the twenty-first-century level. We cannot possibly produce at the rate culture is telling us we should. We were not made to carry the weight of the world, not in our pockets, not in our hearts, not in the delicate architecture that is our nervous system.

I wonder sometimes if one of the primary causes of the prevalent anxiety in our society is our constant, incremental exposure to trauma. While our ancestors had to hold the pain and losses of their family and surrounding communities, we hold the pain of the whole world. Through the news feeds on our phones, we bear witness to global grief. We watch wars unfold thousands of miles away, see buildings crumble in earthquakes, memorize the names of children who are killed by gun violence, hear their mothers weeping. As Christians, we feel compelled to fix it all, to somehow make it better. Emotionally, spiritually, and physiologically, it is a lot to bear up under.

Wendell Berry once wrote: "There can be no such thing as a

'global village.' No matter how much one may love the world as a whole, one can live fully in it only by living responsibly in some small part of it."[7] The grace of my body is that it situates me in a particular country, in a particular state, in a particular community, in an actual home. There may be seasons where we serve overseas or travel to far-flung corners of the world for a specific purpose. But wherever I am, the body forces me to be present, not omnipresent. The body is a beautiful border.

It takes a lot of strength to know your limits, to admit to yourself what you *can* do and what you *cannot* do. It is okay, sometimes, to turn off the TV, to put your phone down, to step away from all the things demanding your physical and emotional energy. It's okay to pay attention to the smallness of your life, to the parameters of your energy. Be present with the people across the street and under your roof, the ones who actually need your undivided attention. Walk the land that is yours. Love your *actual* neighbor. Caretake your corner of the world. Be present in your community. Proximity is enough. It is okay to say it is all you can do. Physiologically, it *is* all you can do. Know the borders and boundaries of your own life, your own body. Contrary to what we've been taught to think, a limit is a blessing. A limit does not confine as much as it defines. It creates identity, clarity, and demarcation.

Treating your body well is an act of humility. It is also an act of self-dignity. To release your pride and admit you need sleep, healthy food, and movement is to remember that your body is fragile, that it needs to be nurtured and protected. To love a body that is in pain or a body that doesn't meet the world's standards of goodness is an act of defiance. It is an assertion of your own worth before God. I must respect my body—as God does—for its inherent value, not simply for its attractiveness or productivity. I recall that when God made humankind, he made us to be caretakers of the world. As my brother-in-law Daniel Evans once wrote, "Some days making the world just a little bit better is resting my weary body. My body is part of the world."[8] We steward creation by stewarding ourselves.

To experience a miracle, to live your life in the aftermath of one, is to exist forevermore in the shadow of a divine expectation. It is both gift and curse. "Well, I suppose God let me live for a reason!" I remember the unabated presence of that thought in the years after my hospitalization. I'd walk the streets of New York City, looking for a soul to save, a fine thing to savor, a good deed to do. I went to the mission field. I signed up to work with the economically disadvantaged. I gave ten years of my life to humanitarian aid. It's not that I'm particularly altruistic. I'm just a person making payments on a gift I could never repay.

That miracle has been my origin story in many ways. If God saved me for a reason, then I am forever looking for *that reason*, and nothing is ever enough. My work, my writing, my kids, my friendships, my efforts…none of these things ever feel sufficient. I am forever feeling the imaginary need to justify being the daughter who lived, the one who was given a second chance at health and happiness.

One of the hardest things I've ever done is learn to love my body for what it is rather than begrudge it for what it is not, to honor its mystery and fragility as much as its predictability and strength. The truth is, even in our weakest moments, our bodies are amazing. They do *so much* for us! Every second, my body produces twenty-five million cells. If my blood vessels were made into a road, that road would take me one hundred thousand miles, just over four times around the globe.[9] It is no small miracle that our hearts beat and our lungs inflate without thought, even when we are sleeping. Our tongues taste sweetness; our eyes take in beauty; our ears vibrate with the sound waves of symphonies. Our bodies are absolutely beautiful.

I want to think more kindly toward my body, to love the skin I'm in. I want to celebrate its successes rather than obsess over its perceived failures. My body has survived, has carried me through so much: illness, infertility, pregnancy, grief, and trauma. It has allowed me to love, to be loved, to serve, and to experience the world. Even in my weakness, I am wonderfully made. Even in my weariness, there is divine strength—the very breath of God— written on my DNA. To *be* in a body is to exist by decree of the Creator. To *be* in a body is to be blessed.

Contrary to what the emotional prosperity gospel would have us believe, we do not need a miraculous story of healing to be thankful for our bodies. We do not need an eye-catching "transformation" via some fad diet to celebrate our bodies. We do not need some superhuman feat of strength to believe that the skin and bones God gave us are enough.

My physicality, the unique and particular way in which I take up space in this world, is God's good and specific design. It is not just my mind or soul that was created good. My body is good too. It is indeed impacted by the fall just like the rest of creation that waits and groans for its redemption. But it is still a good gift. I breathe as only I can breathe, move as only I can move, exist as only I can exist. I *can* love the skin God gave me. He gave it to *me* as my home. My rest.

And in that rest, God seems to whisper, "I didn't save you so you could save the world. I've already done that." I've begun to think he saved me so I could savor the world, savor *his* saving of it. I think he saved me so I could simply be a witness to the miracle—not the miracle of my good health, but the miracle of existence. The miracle of grace.

A BLESSING:
Humility

*Do nothing out of selfish ambition or vain conceit. Rather,
in humility value others above yourselves, not looking to your
own interests but each of you to the interests of the others.*

*In your relationships with one another, have the same
mindset as Christ Jesus:*

Who, being in very nature God,
   did not consider equality with God
something to be used to his own advantage;
rather, he made himself nothing
   by taking the very nature of a servant,
   being made in human likeness.
And being found in appearance as a man,
   he humbled himself
   by becoming obedient to death—even death on a cross!
—Philippians 2:3–8

What simmers at the center of all my efforts to find my calling, to build community, and to serve God with all my strength is a desperate yearning to be seen. To be known. To be recognized and revered. Selfish ambition and vain conceit are symptoms of a deeper rot, the same decay that crept in at the edges of Eve's heart when the Serpent first told her lies about her lack. *This is not enough*, my soul murmurs. To play by the rules, to do my duty and be faithful—it is not sufficient. I want accolades. I want belonging. I want to leverage my acts of righteousness to my advantage, to use them to garner affirmation and praise.

Jesus knew we would all struggle with a fear of anonymity, a fear of lowliness. And so, before he became the ultimate example of lowliness by laying down his life, he offered us *words* of lowliness. He showed us the *way* of lowliness. In a world where self-discovery is our highest virtue—where influence and attention are our most prized outcomes—Jesus offers us a radical alternative: the self-emptying freedom of humility.

"Be careful not to practice your righteousness in front of others to be seen by them," Jesus preached in the Sermon on the Mount. "If you do, you will have no reward from your Father in heaven" (Matt. 6:1). He tells the listeners how they *ought* to give to the poor—with similar instructions on prayer and fasting. We must do it in a way that is hidden:

> So when you give to the needy, do not announce it with trumpets, as the hypocrites do in the synagogues and on the streets, to be honored by others. Truly I tell you, they have received their reward in full. But when you give to the needy, do not let your left hand know what your right hand is doing, so that your giving may be in secret. Then your Father, who sees what is done in secret, will reward you. (vv. 2–4)

There is a world of meaning in the word Jesus uses for "hypocrites," the people who flaunt their good deeds and acts of virtue.

The word for "hypocrite" was often used in ancient Greek culture to describe a masked actor in a drama played out onstage.[1] These were thespians skilled in the art of performance, and in the art of disguise.

It is a sad fact that virtue too often demands an audience. As a little girl, I was given ribbons for memorizing Scripture and lollipops for singing a hymn or praying a prayer onstage at my church. As I've grown older, almost every job I've ever had has been at a Christian institution of some kind: a Christian college, a Christian nonprofit, a Christian aid organization, a Christian publisher. My career trajectory, my pay rate, and my social standing have almost always been tied in some way to my spirituality, my religious performance. I guess that makes me a professional Christian. Spending your entire life in the Christian subculture is both a blessing and a complication for your walk with God. It's easy to inadvertently commodify your faith, leverage it for your own advancement.

This proclivity toward performance is most certainly exacerbated by social media. The platforms we use to connect with the world incline us toward grandstanding. These sites, and the time we spend on them, are not merely a distraction—they are reforming our anthropology and rewiring our brains. We have become a human race of exhibitionists, just like those actors on the Greek stage. We move through our days looking for content to post, longing for someone to bear witness to our lives.

Jesus says that the people who engage in acts of righteousness to be seen by others will have their reward in full. But the reward of worldly affirmation is like empty calories. Like junk food and diet soda, the approval of others will trick your soul for a moment into thinking it is full, that it's gotten something good. But you will soon find that you cannot live off this superficial sustenance. You cannot survive on it. Your character will eventually wither, waste away for want of the real, sustaining abundance of the presence of God. Pastor and author Scot McKnight says of those who seek worldly recognition: "You got the good you wanted, but what you wanted was not good."[2]

Meanwhile, Jesus reminds us that God resides in the hidden places. There is a secrecy required of the Christian life, a call to embrace anonymity and pay close attention to the motivations and desires that grow in the dark soil of our unseen souls. Dallas Willard writes, "If we would walk with Him, we must walk with Him at that interior level."[3]

When I look back on the life of Jesus, I see a man who made every effort to live this kind of quiet and humble existence. He was well into adulthood before he began drawing a crowd with his miraculous deeds. He even seemed hesitant to perform his first miracle; his mother, eager to help her friends, had to convince him to turn water into wine. Scholars have long been mystified by what some call the Messianic Secret, a motif in the gospel writings in which Jesus seems to direct his followers to keep his identity as the long-awaited Savior and healer confidential.[4] This cloaking of power, the veiling of authority that is so often chosen as the garb of God, puzzles me. Perhaps because he knew he'd be asking us to embrace the same humility, Jesus wanted to show us it was possible. He wanted to show us *how*.

Emblazoned on the North Carolina state seal is the Latin phrase "esse quam videri," which means "to be, rather than to seem." This, to me, feels like a sermon in and of itself, one that stares down my soul every time I fill out paperwork at the DMV, get something notarized, or ride in an elevator. I've spent my entire life striving to *seem* a certain way to people. But what Jesus is telling us in the Sermon on the Mount is that a truly blessed life requires no audience. Character that is truly godly is satisfied to simply *be*.

When Jesus says that we should not let our left hand know what our right hand is doing as we serve, I wonder if this is his miraculous way of speaking to that inner part in all of us, that part where the self-analysis and self-scrutiny won't stop. Jesus himself says "enough" to the Sisyphean task of earning our own righteousness, of proving our goodness to others and, more importantly, to ourselves. "Stop watching yourself," Jesus begs us. Stop being your own greatest admirer. And stop being your own harshest critic. Be at rest. Just *be*.

Will we ever truly believe in the deep, abiding blessing of humility? Humility, which is notoriously lacking in the ancient Greek virtues, is the great gift of our faith. It is the crown jewel in the regalia of Christian virtues. It makes all other virtues possible. It enables me to see others—even those who are different from me—as truly valuable. It allows me to exist in this commercialized world as a human, not just as a consumer or a commodity. Christian humility allows *God's* love to do the work of securing my ego. It allows me to fail without losing face, to be wrong without surrendering my worth. It allows me to be physically weak and still maintain my inner strength. It allows me to be unnoticed or unremarkable and still keep my dignity. It calls me to believe that God is enough.

Jesus tells the story of a man who struggled to believe that God was enough. He was the oldest son of a wealthy landowner. The good son. The faithful son. He had a younger brother who was a scoundrel, a rebel who had the gall to ask for his inheritance prematurely and then wasted it all on wild living: gambling, drinking, and prostitutes. Meanwhile, the older son stayed home and carried out his duty. He served his father, worked hard for the family, and lived righteously.

In an epic plot twist, the rebellious younger brother returned home broke, starving, and desperate. Thinking perhaps his father would show him mercy and allow him to work as a hired hand, he humbled himself. He came limping down the road home prepared to grovel and repent. Instead, the father ran to embrace him and threw an enormous party for the unfaithful son, celebrating him with the entire household. He put a luxurious robe around him, decked him out with a fancy ring and shiny new shoes. They killed the fattened calf and cooked up a great meal.

Meanwhile, the older brother was working away in the fields just like he always had. The fields were where we first met him, where he was likely weary from a long day of labor, from the cost of duty. As he was wrapping up his work for the evening, he heard the sound of music and dancing coming from the house. A servant informed him that his reprobate brother had returned and that the father was throwing a big party for him.

The older brother was filled with rage. He was so angry that he refused to go inside, didn't even care to see his brother who had been gone so long. The father went out to meet the older brother, pleading with him to come inside and rejoice with him. But the older son was unmoved in his bitterness: "Look!" he cried out. "All these years I've been slaving for you and never disobeyed your orders. Yet you never gave me even a young goat so I could celebrate with my friends" (Luke 15:29).

Angry because he longed to be celebrated. Angry because he needed his friends to know he was a favored son. Angry because he wanted the entire household to esteem his righteousness. Angry because he wanted to be seen.

The father replied with one of the most heartfelt and heartbreaking statements in all of Scripture: "My son," he said, "you are always with me, and everything I have is yours" (v. 31). The only emotion more palpable in this text than the older brother's rage is the father's deep, deep sadness. It is as if he is asking, "Am I not enough, my son? Do you really need all that recognition? It is not enough just to *be with me*?"

C. S. Lewis once said, "He who has God and everything else has no more than he who has God only."[5] Our Father knows our secrets. He knows who we truly are, and he loves us just the same. We don't have to jump up and down, waving our arms. We do not have to yell. We are seen. We will not disappear. The truth of our enduring, immutable belovedness paradoxically buoys the ego and subdues the pride. We matter because he says so. He has written his divine imprint on our very being, sealed our identity as his children. We are valuable because he values us. *His* image is the only image we need.

"The Theater of God is in the hidden corners," John Calvin once said.[6] The humility of hiddenness is an unfamiliar virtue not only to the ancient Greeks. It is unfamiliar to me. But when I am really, truly quiet, God calls me there. To that secret place, the place where I hear him whisper:

You are always with me.

All I have is yours.

And it is more than enough.

PART 3

CHAPTER 7

SANCTUARY

(Go to Church)

A year and a half after the start of the pandemic, I found myself sitting alone in a church pew, my hands sweaty and my heart racing. Our worship leader was finishing up the last song of the praise set, and it was almost time for me to walk up on the stage to deliver some announcements and a homily. I fumbled with the lapel mic and skimmed my notes one last time, but the words were all a blur.

I can't do this, I thought to myself, scanning the room for the fastest route to the exit.

I don't normally get nervous about public speaking. But the nature of my announcement and homily were inching me closer and closer to a full-blown panic attack that morning. Our church was experiencing the same pandemic challenges plaguing many churches in America: changes in staffing, decreased engagement and giving, burnout among leaders, the tension between staying open and staying safe. As a member of our leadership team, I'd agreed to stand in front of the church and share our plan for a way forward in light of those changes and challenges. And, somehow, to make a case for why people should stay. Why they should not give up.

Sitting there that morning, though, I was burdened by a profound awareness of the difficulties we were facing beyond just pandemic hardships. I felt the rising tide of disillusionment and outrage with the Church at large. Across Christianity in America and beyond, sex abuse scandals, toxic pastoral leadership, lack of accountability, racial injustice, platforming and consumerism, Christian nationalism, and degrading misogyny were being exposed like never before.

The outcry on social media and the empty pews across America are a scathing indictment of the Church. Studies show that only 29 percent of Americans regularly attend Sunday services now, and that percentage is even smaller among millennials and Gen Z.[1] While there are countless historical and sociological reasons why participation in traditional religious settings is dwindling, many have left the Church because they feel hurt, taken advantage of, and misled. They are walking away wounded and scarred. That morning, the swell of resentment felt so real and crushing to me it was as if a literal wave were surging up around my chest. My *own* hurts and disappointments threatened to pull me under.

Some say it is a season of reckoning for the American Church, a revelation of sorts. There's something to be said for a good old-fashioned apocalypse, for the winnowing and refining that ensue in its wake.

But as for me, I felt too weary for winnowing. I felt like I didn't have the reserve or fortitude to steady my soul through an apocalyptic unveiling. I was hurting and tired after years of losses and a disorienting pandemic. I was confused and overwhelmed by the division all around us. I wanted the Church to carry me, to ease my burden, to tell me what I should do and what I should think. I wanted church to be a sanctuary. Instead, it felt like the Church itself was swinging a wrecking ball at me. My theology, my confidence in the people of God, and my hope for the Church all felt at risk of demolition.

For so long, the Church had been my mother. She had raised me, had cared for me, had sent me out into the world. And now, it felt like I was learning that my mother was absent, unfaithful, unstable, and careless. Maybe she had been all along, and I just hadn't had the eyes to see it.

I looked around me at the walls and chairs and faces that made up my own small church. How was I supposed to get in front of these folks—a community that was running short on resources and morale—and ask them not to quit? How could I impart hope when I was losing *my* hope for the future of the Church? How was I supposed to ask *them* to stay when *I* was considering leaving myself?

"God, help me," I prayed through tears as I walked to the front. "Please. *Help me to stay.*"

I always write and speak about the Church with a healthy dose of fear and trembling. Depending on the crowd you are addressing, you can be eviscerated for either speaking critically of the Church *or* speaking kindly of it. There are those who will say that the Church is rotten to the core, that as an institution, it has so weaponized words like "repentance," and "grace," and "hope" that we must reinvent an entirely new language to engage in conversation about spiritual matters. They will say there's nothing left to do but burn everything down and start again.

There are others who will cling relentlessly to the old vestiges of the Church, asserting that she is the chosen instrument of God to bring about his kingdom in this world. Lauding her as the bride of Christ, they will condemn you for uttering any word of slander or disdain against her. They will protect her reputation at all costs.

I'll speak transparently and say that I've found myself somewhere in the middle. I've attempted to find a path that makes space for both the scrutiny of and tenderness toward the Church or, at the very least, makes space for hope. I recognize that it is likely my privilege that allows me to journey in this way. I had a fairly positive experience growing up in religious institutions. This is due most certainly to the wise discernment of my parents, who always made sure we attended churches that were, for the most part, free of strangling legalism and unhealthy leadership. The churches I was part of in my childhood were grace-filled communities, where curiosity was welcome and pastors were humble. I was affirmed and cherished in these spaces and that, of course, has made all the difference. Sometimes, I joke that I have American evangelicalism survivor's guilt because I was spared much of the dysfunction and abuse that have occurred in so many churches.

I also recognize that I had the benefit of being the kind of person who generally feels safe in church. I was a well-behaved, polite, and rather quiet girl who had no aspirations to lead—or as some would say, "subvert male authority." From my vantage point, church was a sanctuary, inviting and secure. I liked it that way. And it took me a while to understand that *my* experience of the Church was not everyone's experience of the Church.

I suppose the only drawback of having had such a privileged, positive experience in an institution like the Church is that it sets some pretty high expectations going forward. Everything I'd witnessed led me to believe that the Church was perfect by design—a good establishment made up of good people. I had all the confidence in the world that going to church would lead to spiritual prosperity, that it would make me happy, make my life better somehow.

It wasn't until I became an adult and started choosing churches for myself that I began to experience deep wounding in communities of faith: leaders who didn't allow for questions, institutions that worked staff and volunteers to the bone, and friends who turned their back on me when my faith no longer fit their mold. This is not the place for recounting all the details of those heartaches. But the hurts and deceptions left me with the distinct feeling of having been duped, like I'd had the wool pulled over my eyes. This place—the Church—is not safe after all!

And it wasn't just the personal grievances. I was also growing in my understanding of ways the Church throughout history has harmed people on the margins, the way it has given in to consumerism and materialism, the way it has allowed those in power to take advantage of the trust and earnestness of the people in their care. One of the hardest parts of these realizations was seeing how hesitant many in the evangelical church have been to admit to these past mistakes and to make an effort to repair what has been broken.

For some reason, many followers of Jesus seem hell-bent on maintaining an "us versus them" mentality—"us" being Christians and "them" being non-Christians. Maybe it's because human beings are drawn to the drama of a fight or the heroics of martyrdom. Perhaps we crave the predictability of homogeny and the bonds of ideological tribalism. Whatever the case, I was always given the impression that the enemy was on the *outside*, that we must valiantly defend the fortress of the faith from the adversaries who sought to destroy us with their secular beliefs and moral bankruptcy.

No one ever told me the enemy might be on the *inside*. I knew wolves prowled around in sheep's clothing, but I had no idea they'd be so effectively disguised. Predators make their home in even the safest of sanctuaries. It's strange how the institution so determined to indoctrinate me with a sound theology of suffering never once admitted that it might be the very source of my suffering.

What exactly *is* the Church? What is its mission, its reason for being? What is the difference between the universal, "capital *C* Church" and the local, "lowercase *c* church"?

The problem with examining that question through the lens of our twenty-first-century American culture is that there is a very specific way we think about entities and enterprises. It's almost impossible for us not to think of the Church as a business. Reflexively, we want to know the mission statement, the target audience, the customer base, and the product being sold. We think of a church in terms of budget and its registration as 501(c)(3). We think of the Church as an industry, an institution, or an establishment.

But the organism that arose in the aftermath of the death and resurrection of Jesus was no monetary enterprise. It was a movement, not a market endeavor. Its growth strategy had nothing to do with profit or platform or the personal success of its leaders. It was a Holy Spirit–driven response to the call of God.

The word for "Church" in the New Testament is *ekklesia*, which means "the assembly." The same word is used interchangeably to describe the local and the universal Church. It is never used to refer to a building. In the Greek, it is not necessarily a religious word, and it had no connotation of institution, organization, or society. It simply meant a gathering of people, a meeting, a congregating.[2]

But there is something holy about this assembly, this groundswell of souls being drawn together to the kingdom of God. It is an assembly gathered by God himself. The simplicity of the term, to me, acknowledges the humanity of it. *Ekklesia* is not merely some impersonal institution or theoretical system. It is a collection of individuals joined together to form a whole, unionized under the call of Christ. We are, as Peter writes in his epistle, "living stones… being built into a spiritual house" (1 Pet. 2:5).

It is no small miracle that the modest beginnings of the Church grew into the global movement it is today. There was nothing about the early Church that was marketable or appealing by the standards of the surrounding culture. A second-century philosopher and opponent of the church, Celsus, mockingly wrote this:

> In some private homes we find people who work with wool and rags, and cobblers, that is, the least cultured and most ignorant kind. Before the head of the household, they dare not utter a word. But as soon as they can take the children aside or some women who are as ignorant as they are, they speak wonders…If you really wish to know the truth, leave your teachers and your father, and go with the women and the children to the women's quarters, or to the cobbler's shop, or to the tannery, and there you will learn the perfect

life. It is thus that these Christians find those who will believe them.[3]

Women and children indeed. The Church was born in the margins. It owes its very existence to the stubborn persistence of ordinary people who were naive enough to go all in on a grace that can't be bought and a love that can't be sold, a kingdom built not by wealth or power or platform, but by humility and servanthood. Christianity and consumerism have *always* hit an impasse. The Church and state have always had a tumultuous relationship because faith, while it is a force, was never meant to be *en*forced. It was meant to be shared, offered, and embraced with humility.

It was this embodied grace, love, and gentleness that served as the gravitational pull that assembled the people we call the Church. But that assembly eventually gave in to the temptation of money and power. It became an establishment and eventually became an imperial institution. The goodness of an institution or system—be it democracy or capitalism or the Church—wholly depends on the goodness and integrity of the people within that institution or system. The Church is a human assembly; therefore, sin is always crouching at the door. Brokenness is always the very real and present possibility.

My friend Mike, who is a pastor at our church, warns me against thinking too idealistically about the early Church. I used to think the story of Acts in the New Testament was a narrative of an idyllic time in the history of the faith, where Christians were all living and thinking as they ought. Instead, in his teaching series on the book, Mike has helped me see that the Church we meet in the pages of Acts is actually full of failure. If Acts is utopia, it is utopia being exploited. Self-serving Ananias and Sapphira leverage the generosity of their fellow believers to boost their own reputations, claiming altruism but secretly withholding resources. Simon the Sorcerer, newly converted, tries to purchase the power of the Holy Spirit with money. Crowds who hear the gospel in Lystra attempt to elevate Barnabas and Paul to godlike status, calling them Zeus and Hermes and offering sacrifices to them. Racism rears its ugly head in the churches of Judea when they hear that Peter has dined with a Gentile. Paul and Barnabas argue about a fellow believer, Mark, and his fitness for duty, eventually parting ways over the dispute.[4]

When it comes to the marketability of the Christian metanarrative, the Bible does itself no favors. It does not present us with appealing, infallible protagonists to root for or inspire us. Its main characters are remarkably human—flawed and prone to corruption: Adam and Eve ate of the forbidden fruit, Moses never made it to the promised land, Joseph's arrogance led to the breakdown of a family, David was a murderer and an adulterer, and Peter was unprincipled and temperamental, denying Jesus at the very moment when courage was most needed. In these fallen heroes we see sins so egregious that if these people were alive today, they'd never be able to show their faces on social media again.

The Bible never sugarcoats these failures. It seems unembarrassed by its own heroes' propensity to become the villain. There are no hushed tones in Scripture, no pretending for the neighbors that the people of God are some perfect, happy family. You could even argue that it is precisely the failings of the people of God that are the linchpin of the story. One of the core narrative arcs of Scripture is the faithlessness of saints. But the persistent counternarrative of the Bible is God's *faithfulness*. He does not repay infidelity with rejection. He is astoundingly kind. His patience toward his people is the very picture of divine love's resilience. Again and again, they leave him. Again and again, he comes after them. It is God's love that inspires, not human performance or personal perfection.

In the Bible, the people of God sometimes face a threat from the outside—pagan warlords or persecution from the Roman Empire. But most of God's sternest warnings are addressed to the people on the inside: Israel, who was in a covenantal relationship with God yet neglected the poor and bowed down to idols. The hypocritical Pharisees, who knew the truth, but deep down were whitewashed tombs. The churches in the province of Asia—whose sins are exposed in the book of Revelation.

If I ever expected the Church to be perfect, it was because I wasn't paying attention to these stories. If I ever thought that Christians were always safe and trustworthy, I'd underestimated the tenacity of sin in the human heart and in human systems. If I thought that the assembly of God's people would always make me happy, then I'd placed my confidence in an institution that was flawed simply because it was made up of flawed people.

Dr. Richard Spencer, a former professor of the New Testament at Appalachian State University, likes to say that Christianity is not a story of transaction. It's a story of *struggle*.[5] The name Israel literally means "to struggle with God." It was the name God gave to Jacob after their tussle in the wilderness in Genesis chapter 32. As the story goes, Jacob and God wrestled at night, after Jacob had been left alone on the long journey back to his homeland. During the match, God saw that he was not prevailing against Jacob, and for some reason, that didn't seem to bother God one bit.

"I will not let you go unless you bless me," Jacob insisted of God (Gen. 32:26), and I can almost see the yearning and obstinance in his face. Jacob, who had done things his own way from the start—who had deceived his father to get a blessing, who cheated his brother to get a blessing, who had spent his whole life bullheadedly striving for the prosperity and the love and the inheritance he wanted—was now *demanding* a blessing from God himself. In spite of his insufferable behavior, I can't help but admire Jacob's determination, the scrappy resolve and hard-nosed grit that grief, disappointment, and failure had infused in him.

It is almost beyond comprehension that God gives in. Shockingly, God *does* bless Jacob. The blessing is the new name—Israel: "because you have struggled with God and with humans and have overcome" (v. 28). Jacob sees God face-to-face and the encounter leaves him with a limp. It seems to me that the people of God have been limping along ever since.

We have seen God, and we lived to tell the tale. We have strived and struggled and clawed for the blessing that was always ours to begin with. Jacob is our father and both his faults and his fortitude live on in our DNA. We have overcome threats from the inside and outside, have survived strife and self-sabotage.

If there is one thing I've learned, it's this: Do not underestimate the Church. She is the underdog by design. And God always seems to be on the side of the underdog.

The call to accept and even embrace the imperfection of the Church is not a call to abdication. Quite the opposite. Accepting that the Church is prone to failure demands action. Tim likes to say that one of the most miraculous things about the Church is that it is self-correcting, or at least it should be. There are certainly times when showing grace might look like letting go, releasing anger, or maintaining patience with the weaknesses in others. Sometimes, we must resist the consumerism and individualism that tempt us to defect at every disagreement and every disappointment.

But staying *with* the Church, loving the Church in the way she needs to be loved, sometimes means challenging powers and hierarchies and demanding change and accountability. *You are the Church*, and sometimes taking care of the Church means taking care of yourself, walking away from a situation that is unsafe or damaging. There is a healthy form of intolerance, a sacred discontent. These necessary disagreements often result in the reforming of the Church.

Raising these concerns and pushing for change come with the risk of being called a gossip or a disrupter. The Church often persecutes its own prophets because the prophecy is hard to hear. "Don't distract from the mission," we are told. But the mission of the Church is not some strategic growth plan or monetary goal. The mission of the Church is not self-preservation. The mission of the Church is to be a light to the world, and the world will never hear our message if we do not have integrity, if we do not have love. Love means holding people accountable for their sinful actions, and this is for the good of the victims as well as the abuser.

If the commitment is to love, then, sometimes, brutally hard conversations are necessary. We must be willing to knock down the pedestals we put our pastors and mentors on. It's hard to hear that someone you trust has failed. It's far too easy to simply maintain a positive outlook, to dismiss failures with trite platitudes: "No one is perfect. We all need grace. God can change their hearts." It's true that no one is beyond the grace of God. But it's also true that no one is above the law. Embracing the idea that the Church is inherently imperfect means agreeing to accept the difficult reality that people can be both helpful *and* harmful. Someone who has significantly impacted your life for the better may very well *also* hurt you irrevocably. And the good someone has done never excuses the bad that they do.

Change is uncomfortable but it is necessary. My dad sometimes compares theological or ideological strains within the Church to the structural design of a tent—and believe me, I've watched my dad struggle to assemble plenty of tents! He says that where there is no tension, the tent collapses.

Where there is no tension within the Church—no challenge, no inquiry, no diversity of thought, no lament, no prophecy—the Church collapses. We've seen this to be true throughout its history.

With tension comes a reinforced refuge, a more enduring shelter. When the imperial Christianity of Constantine threatened the purity of the Church, the desert mothers and fathers fled to the wilderness in search of virtue and community. When papal corruption and works-based righteousness strangled the Church of the Middle Ages, seeds of the Reformation were sown, and in 1517 Martin Luther nailed his Ninety-Five Theses to the door of Castle Church in Wittenberg, Germany.

While the hollow, distant deism of the Enlightenment shaped the religious landscape of early America, revivalists led a series of fervent awakenings that swept across the land and invigorated the

Church. Later, as the wealthy congregations retreated to the safety and prosperity of the suburbs, other Christians got involved in the settlement house movement, offering services to the economically under-resourced in crowded urban centers.[6]

While many white Southern Christians continued to perpetuate the racist legacy of slavery, Black churches mobilized a movement of change, with ministers like John Lewis, Ralph Abernathy, and Martin Luther King Jr. at the helm. In the era of Christian celebrityism, where the protection of power and platforms often leads to abuse of the vulnerable and systematic cover-ups, the #churchtoo movement charges forward. Leaders like Boz Tchividjian and Rachael Denhollander are hard at work bringing greater accountability and meaningful consequences to leaders who exploit their power.

Not all of these corrections have been without error. Sometimes we undercorrect and sometimes we overcorrect. Leaders of even the most righteous resistance movements are flawed too. While some orthodoxies of the Church have been constant, the path of orthopraxy has been a meandering one. If we are willing to take a long view of history, to walk with patience on this wandering path, I believe God will meet us there, will see us safely to the ultimate destination of kingdom.

He is always at work, reforming and refining his Church through the unlikeliest of means. God's story is good not because his people are always good, but because *he* is always good. He animates goodness and mercy within us. We have the privilege of being remade by him over and over, to be born again and again and again. God could have easily imposed the kingdom onto the world with a swift sword or his fierce presence. Instead, he chose imperfect people like you and me to reach other imperfect people.

Much like the choice of the incarnation, God's decision to use human ambassadors is a decision of meekness over might, familiarity over force.

As inspiring as all this sounds, sometimes I still want to grab God by the shoulders, to shake him and scream at him, "What were you thinking?! Why did you ever put humans in charge of anything? Didn't you know we'd mess this up? Didn't you know we'd plunder and grab political power and manipulate your sacred Word to justify all kinds of evil? Didn't you know we would give you a bad name? *Didn't you know?*"

This, I suppose, is a holy frustration. Perhaps it is one of the holiest negative emotions we can ever experience. Every important movement of reformation was born of a holy indignation. Yes, we can acknowledge the reality that the Church is not perfect and make peace with that truth. But accepting that truth doesn't mean we don't fight to make it better every single day.

We must sit with this holy feeling awhile, let it teach us something. In the end, who can argue with a God who is willing to "fail" in the name of love? We are not perfect, but we are the chosen. We are chosen in love. When I let that truth wash over me, I can almost hear God whisper: "Don't give up on the Church. I love her. I love her. I love her."

It has been a difficult decade for those of us still clinging white-knuckled to our hope for the future of the Church. Sometimes I wonder if the reason I've fretted so much about the future of our church here in Boone is because I needed some reassurance or proof that Christianity in America *could* endure. I needed *our*

church to survive because I needed *the* Church to survive. I didn't want it to fail because *I* didn't want to fail.

But I am reminded that the future and goodness of the Church does not depend on any one individual's experience of it. The Church will always exceed a single vantage point. My friend Graham, another pastor at our church, reminds me that our metrics for success and failure too often mirror the metrics of capitalism and consumerism. Too many people like to praise a church for its "good fruit"—and by good fruit they mean growing numbers, shiny facilities, big platform, and massive outreach. This is very often how we justify abuse, dismiss narcissism, and ignore exploitation. "But look at the fruit!" we say. "Surely God's hand is in it."

If shiny programs, lots of money, big numbers, and media attention are what make us happy, then that is an unholy happiness. If that is my only idea of success, I am missing the mark entirely. This is the fruit of consumerism and individualism. It is not the fruit of the Holy Spirit. It is not the fruit of a *true assembly*. The true metric of goodness, simply put, must be *faithfulness*—an unrelenting commitment to Christ and the way of life to which he calls us. As Graham has pointed out to me, plenty of unfaithful churches have been wildly successful by the world's standards. And plenty of faithful churches have not met the world's standards of success, have maybe even had to close their doors.[7]

Whenever I think about—or criticize—the institution of the Church, I, like any Christian, must recognize that *I* am the Church. I have added to its faithfulness and its unfaithfulness. I am one of those living stones, part of that great assembly. I, too, may have contributed to dysfunction and harm within the Church, and so before I denigrate an ambiguous institution, it's wise to evaluate my own complicity. Have I helped to make the Church a true sanctuary?

How would the Church in America be transformed if we measured our success not by our budgets or buying power or attendance but rather by the fruit of the Spirit as spelled out by God in his Word? Love, joy, peace, patience, kindness, goodness, faithfulness, gentleness, and self-control (see Gal. 5:22–23).

Plenty of churches in this country and around the world are producing this kind of fruit in abundance. At our church, we are pursuing it with all our might, and I'm proud of us. It's not always easy. Sadly, it is rarely the quiet, steady faithfulness that makes headlines. The world's attention will always be held rapt by epic failures. We are drawn to a fallen hero, maybe because we recognize ourselves in him.

But God is at work in the lives and through the ministry of gentle shepherds, men and women of the faith who show up every day to bandage the wounded, serve the poor, minister to hurting marriages, condemn exploitation, protect the abused, and exhort others to love and goodness. This *assembly*—this coming together, this building together, this mending together—this is the purpose of the Church, and God has called it good.

That morning at our church, I felt something well up in me as I stepped in front of our gathering and flipped on my lapel mic. Quite suddenly, my anxiety was replaced by resolve. Call it hope or call it determination. Call it an answer to prayer. Maybe call it stubbornness. I felt a wave of new life wash over me, something akin to a baptism or perhaps even a winnowing. I knew in that moment I was not ready to quit.

I still feel like the Church has something beautiful to offer to the world. I still feel like *my* church has something beautiful to offer to the world. I wanted to be part of it, and I wanted to ask others to be part of it too. I still wasn't exactly sure what I should say. But after giving an update on some steps forward, I did all I knew to do. I started talking about history.

I reminded *our* church that *the* Church is two thousand years old, and that its story is even older, with roots reaching back to the faith of Abraham. What began as a group of ragtag rejects, who worshipped a Savior who'd been put to death, and who were violently scattered by persecution, has now become the world's largest religion, with believers in almost every country on earth.

The Church's reach is not confined to the political borders of this nation or to the ideological hostility of our time. The unprecedented growth of Christianity in the Global South has decentered the West from its place of religious power. Around the world, songs of Christian worship reverberate down the narrow corridors of slums, echo across villages, and resound in both palaces and prisons. The Bible has been translated into more than seven hundred languages,[8] its wisdom resonating across cultural, socioeconomic, and generational divides.

The Church has survived persecution, empire, the East-West Schism, plague, pestilence, papal corruption, and the Reformation. It will survive this moment because it is so much bigger than this moment. Plenty of times throughout its history, the Church has been left for dead. But the Church got back up.

God, in his mystifying wisdom, did not set the foundation or

raise the walls of the Church with the glorious, untouchable ala-
baster of heaven. Instead, he built the Church with living stones.
You and me. We are imperfect so the Church is imperfect. Every
time we practice the ancient ritual of the Eucharist, we remember
that the story of the cross began with human betrayal. As the traditional reading goes, "The Lord Jesus, on the night he was betrayed,
took bread" (1 Cor. 11:23). Failure is written into the blueprint of
this building. Still, we take the bread and drink the wine and revel
in the gracious choice to be embraced and commissioned. We go
to church because we know God is slowly transforming it into a
true sanctuary.

The breath of God still blows through these walls, sustaining us,
correcting us, empowering us. Sometimes I think of a world without the Church. If the Church had never been, so much would be
lost. Countless clinics, schools, and nonprofit organizations have
been founded by people of faith. It was the early Church that first
dreamed up the idea of a hospital, a place designed to provide hos-
pitality and care for the sick and dying who had been abandoned
by the rest of society.[9] I think of the works of art, the pieces of
music, the poetry and literature that would be lost because they
were inspired by our sacred texts and resourced by the Church.
And despite their imperfections, Christians are still some of the
likeliest citizens in this country to both adopt children and to give
financially to charities.[10] Christians all over the world are actively
serving in neighborhood initiatives, humanitarian aid, and social
justice.

I know the feeling of wanting to walk away. Sometimes, it
seems like the path of true righteousness actually leads us *away*
from the Church, rather than *to* it. People have tainted the institution of the Church. There will be times we need to burn it down

and build it back. But God is swinging the hammer and nails right along with us. God *will* build his church. Herod couldn't stop it. Caesar couldn't stop it. Our failure and betrayal can't stop it. Even hell won't prevail against it—though I'm certain it has tried. The Church will survive this moment. *We* will survive it. Again and again, God redeems the call of the *ekklesia*, reforms and restores its assembling.

And come hell or high water, by his grace, we *will* get our blessing.

CHAPTER 8

SUFFERING
(Find Peace and Purpose in Pain)

The very first time I set foot in India, I went as part of a tsunami relief group from the Christian college I was attending. It was early 2005 and just weeks earlier, on Boxing Day, a magnitude 9.1 earthquake, one of the largest in recorded history, ruptured a fault line stretching nine hundred miles just off the coast of Indonesia. This triggered a hundred-foot wave that devasted the coastal regions of countries across South Asia and East Africa. It is estimated that almost 230,000 people were killed. It was one of the deadliest natural disasters in modern history.[1]

I remember being glued to the television over the New Year's holiday. Like everyone, I was trying to make sense of why God had allowed something so horrific to happen. As details emerged about the lives lost and the communities destroyed, I felt desperate to do something, to give my feet and hands a task in response to the misery I was seeing.

The opportunity to serve came in the form of a spring break mission trip with some of my classmates. A professor of ours had a contact in India, Augustine, who had teams working in some of the coastal villages that had been hit by the wave. The plan was to connect with him in Chennai and travel together to some seaside communities farther south where we would visit victims and assess the needs.

Three months after the tsunami, some of the impacted towns had begun to clean up and rebuild. But the grief lingered heavily in the air. Photographs of lost loved ones adorned with marigolds were displayed everywhere, and names of the missing were scrawled on seawalls and sidewalks. Looking back, I realize we were not exactly there to help. We were there to bear witness. Augustine needed privileged Westerners to experience the heartache in person so that we could tell our friends and family back home. He needed the world to hear, to care, and to give generously. He and his teammates would remain behind and carry out the real labor of loving, serving, and rebuilding.

I remember walking in between two small huts and happening upon a woman who was sitting and crying on a mat. I slowly bent down toward her. She grabbed my shoulders, thrusting a picture of her little girl into my hands, all the while moaning aloud. Her daughter was missing, presumably swept away into the ocean the day of the wave, never to be seen again. She was speaking Tamil, so I couldn't understand a word she was saying. But hers was wild and untamed grief like I had never experienced before in America. In a matter of seconds, I was sobbing, too, embracing her, and telling her how beautiful her daughter was.

It was a moment I'll never forget. Surrounded by rubble and trees stripped bare by the waves, death was palpable. *This is real*, I thought to myself and shuddered. *It's not just something that happened on TV.*

As the light faded, Augustine found us and signaled that it was time to leave. One of his colleagues stayed behind, though, and spoke to the woman for a while. I looked back and watched them for a moment and my breath caught in my throat as I realized he might be sharing the gospel with her. In a country where the vast majority are Hindu, this may have been the first time she was hearing the story of Jesus.

I silently rejoiced as our van made its way back to the guesthouse that night. Suddenly, the tragedy of the tsunami made sense to me. A wave of relief washed over me as I thought of all the people who may have a chance to hear the gospel because of this terrible catastrophe. Praise God! I had my *reason*; I'd discovered the purpose for the pain. I'd witnessed the divine redemption and could now explain *this* particular problem of suffering. I imagined that woman would be feeling better in no time. I know I sure did.

I flew home from that disaster zone back to the safety of my spring semester with my neatly structured theology in place, a tidy bow wrapped around a calamity. I'd gotten the miracle I needed to feel at peace about this unspeakable tragedy. My mission trip had been a success. At least it had been for me.

And now I don't know whether to scold, scoff, or pity the person I was. She was clueless. I resent her in some ways, am embarrassed by her.

And also, sometimes I wish she could have stayed that way forever.

Ce ~

There is something in all of us that longs to understand why the world is the way it is, especially when we encounter pain. Attempting to explain how an all-powerful, all-good God could allow suffering in the world is no new effort. Everyone from Irenaeus in the second century, to Saint Augustine in the fourth century, to Hegel in the early nineteenth century, and countless others have attempted to resolve the problem of evil with a well-crafted theodicy, a vindication of God and his actions.

Most of us aren't philosophers. Yet, we are still plagued with a deep desire to understand, to make sense of our sorrow. The musings of dead theologians and Sophists don't help much when you are in the throes of grief. But we patch together our own explanations or theories, perhaps as a way of pushing back against the feeling of helplessness that comes with an encounter with death or loss.

I suppose it's understandable that, when faced with the wily and unpredictable wilderness of suffering, we try to make a map. We attempt to establish landmarks and reorient ourselves. We rationalize how we got here and negotiate a way out. We insist that God give us a compass where the true north is a just world, where good things happen to good people and bad things happen to bad people.

Sometimes, we litigate our own culpability, wallowing in shame thinking that we may have done this to ourselves. If prosperity is a sign of God's approval, then pain can very easily be misconstrued as a metric to measure his disdain. Other times, we seethe in anger toward the person or institution we perceive as liable: a family member, a friend, the Church, or the government. We tell the origin stories of our agony. We try to get out ahead of the next catastrophe.

Isn't that the story of Job? It is a tale of a group of friends who start off well with their silence but spend the rest of the book fumbling to decode the mystery of Job's misfortune in the form of lengthy speeches and pompous rhetoric. God allows the conversation to continue for an exceptionally long time. I used to get annoyed with these wise guys and their verbose dialogue. But then, I went through a season of my own suffering and realized the text of Job sounded a whole lot like the rambling monologue in my own head.

We are no different than Job and his friends. We need to believe that everything happens for a reason, and we feel entitled to know that reason. *This happened because you sinned. This happened because someone else sinned. This happened because you were not in the center of God's will. This happened because God is angry with you. This happened because our nation has strayed from God. This happened because there is so much evil in the world.*

Because. Because. Because.

And after we've found the reason, after we've solved the equation and discovered the cause, we need to know the effect. We must identify the silver lining or redemption story. *This happened so that you would learn to trust God more. This happened so that you would have a wonderful testimony to share with the world. This happened so that you would grow spiritually. This happened so that even greater things could come your way. This happened so that you would learn patience. This happened so that God would get the glory.*

So that. So that. So that.

The unavoidable truth, however, is that we cannot always know how or why or for what purpose suffering enters our lives. The book of Job gives us a backstage pass to Job's story of affliction. Job, a righteous and upright man, is struck with calamity because of a diabolical dare. In chapters 1 and 2, we learn that during a meeting of the angelic beings at a mysterious divine council, an adversarial agent—the Satan—challenges God. He proposes that God allow him to strike Job and then watch to see if Job maintains his righteousness. God, confoundingly, agrees. He gives Job over to the Satan, and Job loses everything: his children, his possessions, and his health.

But we often take this insider knowledge for granted. We forget that God never pulls back the curtain for Job himself. Job never learns the reason for his suffering. It remains a mystery to him.

It's not just our fragility that makes us uncomfortable. Modern Americans have lost almost all capacity for mystery. Once you've explored the edges of the world, soared to the brink of outer space, outlined quantum mechanics, and listened to the songs of black holes and dying stars, it's easy to start feeling a bit like God. *If God is all-knowing, then why shouldn't I be? Am I not entitled to the truth?*

We as humans understand death, at least to a degree. We can articulate the physicality of it. We name a cause of death, make a declaration of death, describe the finer details of a body's expiration. But the mystery of mortality is something we'll never be able to fully wrap our minds around. How can a person be so fully present with us one moment, and the next moment, be gone? And it is not only loved ones that are lost. Dreams die too. This is a core truth of human existence: Anything can go sideways at a moment's notice. Even our best-laid plans can come to a crashing halt. Even our most valuable treasures can be taken from us.

Our need to translate our suffering into a moral lesson or a utilitarian purpose reveals our addiction to productivity. It exposes our hunger for agency and control, our desperate longing to write our own ends to our stories. "It is what it is" is somehow never good enough for us. Christians—who make huge claims about their belief in God's sovereignty and their willingness to simply trust and obey—are just as starved for control as anyone else. We are just as eager to know how, and why, and for what.

My brother-in-law Eddie says there is a risk in what he calls "one-verse theology." We find a few instances in Scripture that provide a reason for a particular pain, and then we build that passage into a systematic explanation of *all* suffering. But tragedy can strike for any number of reasons. It *may* be because we've made bad choices. It *may* be because someone else made a bad choice that is negatively impacting us. It *may* be because God is disciplining us. God *may* have allowed suffering in my life to teach me something. He *may* use my story to draw others to himself. He *may* even be negotiating with Satan over the status of my soul.

The problem is that most of the time, we just don't know. The harder calling, the narrow way, is to keep moving forward even when we don't have all the answers or silver linings we desperately want. But that's a hard journey, the uncertainty pressing in at every side, sometimes even suffocating our faith.

For better or worse, during the breezy, beautiful years of my childhood, I developed a very long list of expectations of what suffering would be like. I knew it was possible, inevitable even, that I would meet hardship someday. But I expected that hardship to look a certain way. I expected God to be present with me, and I expected that presence to feel good, reassuring. I expected a peace that passes understanding. Mostly, I expected the redemptive story to present itself to me if not immediately, then in very due course. Like the flip of a switch, the lights would come on. The map would be drawn up and the compass would lead me straight out of the wilderness, out into bright, open air. After all, God would never give me more than I could handle.

Or so I thought.

Ce–꙰

Most people in life experience a "before and after" event, a loss so significant that it rewires their mental and emotional hard drive permanently. That event, for me, happened in my mid-thirties. It was a series of events, really. Over the course of four years, I lost a grandmother I dearly loved, and I had three miscarriages. The most disorienting and catastrophic loss was the unexpected death of my sister.

You can imagine my shock when I realized I *could not*, in fact, handle it. Mere hours after my sister's death, I understood that this thing called grief was much, much different than I thought it would be. My world had spun off its axis and, mentally, I couldn't decipher north from south, east from west. Making a map of *this* wilderness felt like making a map of another dimension. I felt no peace, no joy, no emotional comfort. All I felt was pain. All I felt was confusion. All I felt was lost. The lights did *not* come on. *I cannot exist inside this ache*, I thought to myself. I had no idea how I was going to survive.

Frankly, it was more than humbling. It was humiliating.

What had I done wrong? I'd cultivated a sound theology of suffering, was walking daily with God. I'd surrounded myself with wise counsel and had people around the world praying for me. Where was the peace I was promised? Why didn't I *feel* better?

This was not a disaster zone that I could get on a plane and fly out of. It was not an inspiring tableau of redemptive purpose that I could look upon with relief or joy. I've thought often of that wailing woman I met in India so long ago, how shattered she was three months after her daughter's death. Only this time, it was my pain that was wild and untamed. *This is real*, I thought to myself once again. Grief is the realest thing I know.

And as I've mourned, and cried out to God, and fumbled around in the darkness for answers, I've had a profound realization: No explanation would be adequate. No answer, no matter how true it was, would be enough. No purpose could provide total relief from my pain. Whatever gift was gained by the death of my sister, I would trade it in a million times over to have her back.

I know the great hope of the Christian is that there is ultimately dignity in suffering and meaning in adversity. But when I was at the epicenter of my grief, my soul lost all capacity for meaning and purpose. I had the feeling of being swallowed up, of my entire life disappearing into the darkness.

Ella Wheeler Wilcox in her poem "Solitude" once wrote:

Laugh, and the world laughs with you;
Weep, and you weep alone;
For the sad old earth must borrow its mirth,
But has trouble enough of its own.[2]

Most of us like to be around people who are happy, people whose lives look like the lives we want for ourselves. I had the distinct feeling when I was grieving that some people were offering trite platitudes in hopes I'd just instantly feel better so that *they* could feel better too. Something about sorrow is infectious.

It is an uphill climb to exist as a mourner in our world. It's hard to be honest and open about negative feelings when an entire culture is screaming at you to just stay positive and believe in yourself because happiness comes from within. There is an immense amount of pressure to present ourselves to the world in a certain way. The insistence that we "smile for the camera" is a relatively new one—as is evidenced by the very glum-looking pictures of my great-grandparents hanging on my living room wall. If someone is going to capture *my* likeness, I want that likeness to appear cheerful, controlled, and optimistic.

These days sadness feels an awful lot like defeat. And it is difficult to admit defeat, to concede that sometimes bad things just happen. So, we try and try to make the bad thing less bad. We reframe adversity as good, call pain an "opportunity" and suffering a "blessing in disguise." But I'm not sure we'll ever move forward if we are not honest with others and with ourselves. There are some losses that simply shatter us. There are some heartbreaks that cannot be mended. If we acknowledged, like the ancient Greeks, that tragedy befalls us sometimes by no fault of our own, then perhaps we wouldn't feel such a strong obligation to ourselves to immediately cure the pain. If we believed our happiness was up to fate or to the gods, then maybe we wouldn't feel so humiliated by our unhappiness. If we were willing to admit that we cannot control all our outcomes, then maybe the art of acceptance would come more naturally to us.

Historian Darrin McMahon writes, "Our suffering in its current form goes beyond the simple restlessness and anxiety of longing…that has always haunted human beings. For to that burden we have steadily added another since the age of Enlightenment: the unhappiness of not being happy. Collectively, we possess more than ever before, and still we long, expecting to be happy, and saddened when we are not."[3] If we all have a right to the pursuit of happiness, then does not the responsibility to lay hold of it fall directly on our own shoulders?

Life would indeed be easier if we could boast that all pain was miraculously transformative. I think our determination to name cause and effect is sometimes indicative of our unwillingness to accept that something unequivocally bad can happen even if God is wholly loving and wholly in control. If God is good, then we must make the bad thing good somehow so that our theological structures remain intact.

Logic doesn't always hold up against the complexity of real life. Our equations fail us. Our formulas break down and reasons escape us. We carry blessing, and we carry curse. Life is paradox. It cannot always be categorized. Seemingly competing truths coexist. Humans are not creatures of either/or. We are creatures of both/and. And so is God.[4]

Acknowledging this is, sometimes, a great comfort to me. And sometimes, it fills me with dread.

What is peace?

I'd like to wrap my fingers around it, be able to name it in all its particularity and textures. Is peace not that holy grail of emotional experiences we are all after? Is it not the prized outcome we are all hoping our therapy, self-care, and mindfulness will achieve? Is it not the reason we so often turn to God in times of trouble?

In the past, I've thought of peace as the absence of emotional pain. I thought it was a feeling of comfort, a mental tranquilizer. I was confident that if bad things happened to me, my heart and mind would be like the eye of a great hurricane. While the winds and rain of my circumstances swirled all around me, my internal disposition would maintain calm serenity, clear blue skies, and a quiet atmosphere.

The Greek word for "peace," *eirene*, is derived from the word *eiro*, which means "wholeness." Like the Hebrew word *shalom*, it paints a picture of unity, of all the essential parts of a thing being joined together properly. While it is used to describe well-being of the mind, there is a civic and political undercurrent to the word. It indicates an absence of warfare and is often used to describe an armistice or a restoration of relationship between nations or conflicting groups.[5]

Grief has taught me a lot about peace. Real peace. I am beginning to understand that peace is not the absence of psychological discomfort like sadness, fear, or anger. Rather, I've come to believe it is the ability to endure in right relationship with God and with myself despite the difficult emotions. Uncomfortable or negative feelings are not a sign that God is not near. He is present in the midst of difficult feelings.

Peace *in* my pain begins when I make peace *with* my pain. I must accept it as part of my story. I cannot wish sorrow away, pretend it doesn't exist. I don't have to make the bad thing good. I can allow it to be bad. And I can allow myself to truly hurt. I believe God gives us divine permission to feel what we feel. We do not have to numb or ignore the pain. In fact, he gives us the gift of lament to express our pain, to indulge it to some degree. And through the naming and acceptance of that pain, I am not destroyed. I do not lose myself to it. I do not lose God to it. Lament is perhaps the most powerful form of worship because it makes space for the goodness and majesty of God to exist alongside the very real experience of tragedy and sorrow.

This may be the reason some Christians replace the word "happiness" with "contentment." Unlike happiness, which is usually a response to circumstances in the moment, true contentment is not the absence of sadness or hardship. Contentment is the ability to live with *both* happiness and sadness, with all the pain and all the pleasure life brings our way. Contentment allows joy and sorrow to coexist, to be at peace with one another.

Paul says that God "comforts us in all our troubles" (2 Cor. 1:4). The word used for "comfort" in this verse is *parakalon*, and commentators observe that its translation as "comfort" fails to convey the depth and richness of the concept. *Parakalon*, when applied to the Holy Spirit, is not palliative in nature. It actually means to strengthen, to set upright. It is the same word we use for "fortify."[6] The comfort of God does not diminish the weight of the sadness. Instead, it builds the muscle needed to carry the very heavy sadness.

God's presence makes survival possible. To admit our need for God is a rather ancient concession, one that harkens back to those doleful Greek philosophers who believed fortune was left solely to the whims of the gods. Fortunately for us, our God is not like the fickle, temperamental gods of Greco-Roman antiquity. Ours is a God who cares, who knows us each by name. This radical dependence on the divine is a subversive proposition to offer to a world that values *self*-help above all else.

The prosperity gospel, the emotional prosperity gospel, and the self-help and wellness culture are, in the end, relentless taskmasters. They tell us we must make our own happiness. They tell us we should not be content to merely survive, that we must *thrive*. But to be honest, I am learning that for some people in some seasons, to simply survive is an absolute miracle. It is brave and gorgeous and stunning. Now, when I think of God comforting me, I don't picture a happy feeling. I picture God breathing for me when I can't breathe on my own. His presence makes it so that I do not disappear.

We do a disservice to our pain when we try to minimize it or make it go away. We rob it of its dignity. The strength of my grief is merely a reflection of the strength of my love for the person or dream I lost. I degrade and dishonor that love when I dismiss my sorrow or replace it with feelings that are easier to manage. I need someone to help me carry the beautiful burden of grief, not pretend it isn't real. God is that strengthener, that fortifier, that comforter. When I was knocked to the ground, God set me upright—broken, but still breathing.

Many early Church fathers posited that there is glory in the experience of suffering, so it must be borne with a cheery smile and joyful disposition. While I believe that the ability to find meaning in pain—the capacity to encounter God in our suffering—is one of the great gifts of Christianity, I no longer believe our faith requires us to bury our difficult feelings. I don't believe sadness or acedia is a deadly sin or a deplorable vice. I believe it is the only natural, fitting response to life in this broken world.

God does not dismiss our pain. He calls it forth, beckons it out into the light, illuminates its darkest corners. Minister and author Barbara Brown Taylor writes with admiration about people who "knew how to bear [sorrow] as an ordinary feature of being human instead of some avoidable curse. Watching them ride the waves of their own dark emotions, I learned that sadness does not sink a person; it is the energy a person spends trying to avoid sadness that does."[7]

The most difficult part of grief for me was not grappling with the pain. Rather, it was grappling with the disappointment of the experience of pain. Grief is slow and ill-fitting. It shook my world, like shifting tectonic plates. It was not the refining fire I thought it would be. Some days, I still feel like it simply melted me away.

But somehow, someway, I am still here. God is still here. I survived. Our relationship survived.

Pastor Mike recently reminded me of how Jesus emotionally handled the grief of the cross. He cried out, "My God, my God, why have you forsaken me?" (Matt. 27:46). Jesus, who clearly had a sound theology of suffering, who knew the reason for his death and the glorious purpose of his pain, mourned mightily. What is most stunning about Jesus' experience of adversity is not that he *felt* fine. It's that he *felt* terrible and yet remained devoted to the task before him. He was patient with his pain. He stayed the course. He endured.

And *that* was the narrow path leading to resurrection.

"Wouldn't it be interesting to cultivate a way of being with God and one another that is lean enough to live in the wilderness as long as necessary?" asks Barbara Brown Taylor.[8] She is speaking of something she refers to as "subsistence spirituality," the kind of theology that is best suited for hard living in the wastelands of life. I'm not a backcountry explorer or wilderness trekker, but I've traveled to enough remote and dangerous areas of the world to know that when you go on a trip like that, you pack light. You leave all the unnecessary things behind, the baggage that made sense in your comfortable day-to-day life. You take only what is required for survival: food, water, warm clothing, and simple shelter.

Some people will tell you that theology is unhelpful during times of suffering. I agree that a theological system imposed on a griever as a way of explaining away their pain is indeed harmful. People don't need an academic lecture when they are hurting. They need presence and kindness.

But I've grown a bit weary of the idea that theology is merely rote, intellectual assent. Theology is more than a cold system, more than a framework meant to control. Theology is simply what you know to be true about God, about yourself, and about the world. To be grounded in these realities is incredibly important during times of suffering, perhaps more important than ever before.

But there may be some doctrinal excesses that can be left at home for the time being. A season of suffering is a great time to become a theological minimalist. By this I mean that it may not be necessary to resolve the finer details of eschatology or atonement theory in your moment of crisis. It may not be the best time to decide if you are a Calvinist or an Arminian. It may be better in the wilderness to pack light. Cling to the clearest, simplest, most fundamental truths: God is real and present. He can be trusted. You are loved and redeemed. Resurrection is coming.

One important theological provision I put in my backpack for my journey through the barren, remote wasteland of grief and suffering was this: God is a griever, a Man of Sorrows. In times of trial, many people elevate the theology of God's sovereignty to assuage their fears and put their minds at ease. I understand this, and I see the value in it. But as I've grown and experienced times of true darkness, I have discovered something wonderfully comforting about the mysterious way in which God, too, suffers *even though* he is sovereign.

Ours is a dynamic, interactive, feeling God. Genesis 6:6 tells us that when humankind rebelled, God regretted having ever made man to begin with, that his heart was deeply troubled over their sin and violence. Isaiah 53:3 says the Messiah will be despised, rejected, and acquainted with grief. He will be a suffering servant. In John 11:35, Jesus weeps over the death of Lazarus even though he knows he'll be resurrecting him just a little while later. And in Luke 22:42, in the Garden of Gethsemane, Jesus is so distraught at the prospect of his death on the cross that he begins negotiating with God, asking for another way. Some historians of the early Church believe that the intensity of Jesus' emotions at Gethsemane may have been a liability to the witness and growth of the gospel because the Greco-Roman world so highly esteemed the "noble death."[9] At least Socrates went to his death with his dignity intact, drinking his hemlock calmly and without complaint. The Savior of the Christians is not only a *crucified* Savior. He is a Savior who seemed, at times, emotionally unhinged.

God arguing with God, internally conflicted, weighing his options, angry, filled with sorrow, hurt by the ones he loved. Maybe this is an image of God some people find hard to bow before or praise. But for me, a God who grieves is a God I am *more* willing to trust. His incarnational way of loving us—of bending low, of emptying himself, of submitting himself to pain and even death—for me makes that sovereignty even more glorious, more astounding, more worthy of our awe.

Of course, when life flies off the rails, we want the victorious God! We want the efficacious Lord! We want Jesus on a white horse coming in all his glory into his kingdom and defeating all evil!

But in our suffering, God has also offered to us the Nazarene—a humble carpenter born into a poor, colonized region of the cruel Roman Empire. He offers us Jesus—riding on a donkey, betrayed and abandoned by his friends, crucified in the most shameful of manners. We get the beautiful both: God of the cross and God of the resurrection.

The challenge for the follower of God is to believe and embrace that *he can* be both. God suffers. And God is sovereign. This tells me that even if I never know the reason or purpose for my suffering, something about it is holy. Something about the experience is refining and formational. The way God models suffering gives me permission to embrace the uncomfortable and fervent nature of it. I am allowed to feel what I feel. I don't have to run from negative emotions. They are not a sign that I am weak or unwise or spiritually unfit.

Author and religion analyst Ross Douthat writes, "One man's mystery is another man's incoherence, and the paradoxes of Christian doctrine have always been a source of scandal as well as strength."[10] The scandalous requirement of suffering, made all the more difficult by our productivity-driven culture, is to embrace the mystery of suffering without needing a cause or a reason or a utilitarian purpose. Accept the absurdity that it can be both bad and good, both achingly empty and brimming with possibility for transformation. Mystery may feel psychologically heavy, but when it is fully embraced, it is actually quite light. It is lean. It is an answer unto itself. It is the perfect provision to add to your supply list for wilderness living.

In his book *Lament for a Son*, Nicholas Wolterstorff writes, "Instead of explaining our suffering God shares it." He goes on:

> We're in it together, God and we, together in the history of our world. The history of our world is the history of our suffering together. Every act of evil extracts a tear from God, every plunge into anguish extracts a sob from God. But also the history of our world is the history of our deliverance together. God's work to deliver the world from its agony; our struggle for joy and justice is our struggle to relive God's sorrow.[11]

This is the beautiful mystery that I simply can't walk away from, the one that calls me back again and again. It is the reason my heart continues to insist that God is indeed *good*. I believe in the redemptive work of suffering. I believe it builds character and increases wisdom. God's love is absolutely powerful enough to take a shattered story and remake a life through his grace and his justice. Those are miracles that should be celebrated. That woman I met on the beach in India may have met God in her pain, maybe even because of her pain. But her grief still mattered. A painful past need not be erased for a future to be rewritten by the pen of redemption. There is beauty for ashes. But the fire is never forgotten.

Sorrow is not supposed to be explained away or justified. I believe it is to be endured, not ignored. To allow pain to work its power in our lives, we must lean into it. We must absorb it. It is through the allowance and acceptance of pain that we become acquainted with God in his pain. For me, this has been the great gift of suffering, the peace that transcended my meager understanding: to better know myself, to know God in his sorrow, and mostly to feel deeply known by him.

CHAPTER 9

SANCTIFICATION

(Grow Close to God)

"There's a God-shaped hole in everyone's heart."

If you've spent even just ten minutes within earshot of American evangelicalism in the last fifty years, then no doubt you've heard this much-beloved proverb at least a handful of times. Probably more. The old adage has been wielded by pastors, authors, artists, songwriters, and motivational speakers alike for years. It serves as both a word of solidarity to the believer and a powerful apologetic to the nonbeliever. I'll admit, I, too, found the concept compelling. I clung to it as a reminder that I'd found the secret to a blessed life in God. It was a rallying cry, a call to share the good news of Jesus so that others could experience the joy of salvation and the satisfaction of walking with the Lord.

It's hard to know when the phrase became mainstream, but most trace the origin of the idea back to seventeenth-century French philosopher and Catholic theologian Blaise Pascal. He wrote in *Pensées*—a work penned as a defense of the Christian faith—of the deep human longing for God:

What is it then that this desire...proclaim[s] to us, but that there was once in man a true happiness of which there now remain to him only the mark and empty trace, which he in vain tries to fill from all his surroundings, seeking from things absent the help he does not obtain in things present. But these are all inadequate, because the infinite abyss can only be filled by an infinite and immutable object, that is to say, only by God Himself.[1]

Most American Christians aren't familiar with Blaise Pascal and even fewer have read his work. But the notion that a relationship with God could fill our hearts with happiness is certainly an appealing one. Growing up, I imagined what this "infinite abyss" might look like in the life of a nonbeliever: disconnection, dread, shame, and sadness. I assumed that anyone who had not asked Jesus into their heart was walking around in a constant state of misery. If they appeared happy on the outside, they were simply faking it. I looked instead at the grown-ups at my church and assumed they were happy, optimistic, and filled with peace and purpose. They'd found the secret to a blessed life. *We'd* found the secret. Christianity was the ultimate consolation, the medication to relieve all emotional ailments.

There are plenty of statements floating around in our collective consciousness that are not entirely untrue but that may leave you with a false impression. I'm afraid the "God-shaped hole" statement may be one of them. Something about this axiom and how it was used led me to believe things about Christians and non-Christians that were not exactly correct. As I grew older, I began to notice something unexpected. I saw non-Christians walking around in broad daylight who actually *were happy*! I got to know them, and as it turned out, they liked their jobs, they had friends, and they had solid marriages. They were truly enjoying their lives with a deep sense of contentment and purpose.

So much for the infinite abyss.

On the other hand, I knew plenty of Christians who were *not* happy. They were frustrated, disappointed, and angry. Their marriages were broken, and their souls were weary. Their friendships faltered and their ministries fizzled. They didn't always talk openly about it, but they were not at peace, not content, and not fulfilled. Worst of all, from time to time, I was one of them!

"Why do the wicked prosper?" It's a question that was asked by Job, by the prophet Jeremiah, by King David, and probably by every human who ever lived. It's humbling to watch the people you thought were reprobates thriving, as if truth were a scam and righteousness didn't matter at all. I wonder if the deeper question beneath that query is this: Why am *I* not prospering? Why has holiness not made *me* happy? If I've done everything right and followed all the rules and believed all the right things, then where is the emotional abundance I was promised? Why does God sometimes feel distant and my efforts meaningless? Why do I feel like I'm the one with a hole in my heart?

I've always felt a bit sorry for poor Thomas, whom we meet in the gospel narratives. He is the disciple who always seems to be defined by his moniker "doubting Thomas," even though his moments of resolute conviction far exceed that infamous instance of waffling uncertainty. Maybe I've felt a kinship to Thomas because he's the only disciple whose bones I've actually seen with my own eyes.

I should say I've *allegedly* seen his bones.

According to legend, Thomas left Jerusalem after Jesus' ascension and traveled to India carrying the testimony of Christ's death and resurrection. It is believed that he was martyred, killed with a spear on a hillside just outside Chennai. That hill, the Saint Thomas Mount, is now home to a modest Catholic chapel. Inside the chapel is a glass exhibit illuminated by fluorescent lights, holding a small, ornamental box encasing shards of bone said to belong to Saint Thomas himself.

Augustine took me there one time. We sluggishly climbed the long set of stairs ascending the hill, the sun beating down on us and the heavy, humid air slowing our steps. As we climbed and sweated, Augustine told me that since the arrival of Thomas long ago, Christianity has maintained a persistent presence in southern India, with both Catholic and Protestant churches in almost every community. There are rumors that Thomas traveled as far as China, Indonesia, and even Paraguay.[2]

Augustine and I walked into the white chapel, grateful for the respite from the heat. The atmosphere inside was hushed and solemn. Oil paintings of other saints lined the walls. People were sitting on the simple wooden pews facing the altar, praying silently, the women covering their heads with their saris and dupattas. I pulled my scarf hastily over my head. Augustine brought me over to the display box and whispered, "They say these are the scraps from his bones," but his half grin and mischievous eyes betrayed his own skepticism. I've learned that Protestant Christians in India have even less of a penchant for relics than Protestant Christians in America. I pressed my forehead against the glass and squinted. The shards were *so tiny*, minuscule even. I could hardly see them.

As we made our way back down the hill, we were met by more

waves of pilgrims. Whether or not the bones are authentic, they've inspired thousands of visitors who come to pay homage to a man who overcame his doubts to become one of the greatest missionaries who ever lived. What a wonder!

What I appreciated about the chapel was that it memorialized Thomas's moment of clarity rather than his moment of misgiving. Painted in bright red letters on the white walls of the chapel just above the entrance are the words "My Lord and my God." This sacred statement, uttered by Thomas as he fingered Jesus' scars, is the core truth I imagine the saint would want to be remembered by. Instead, most of us have enshrined him as a cynic. A naysayer. A fear-driven sellout.

Elsewhere in the Gospel of John we see Thomas acting as an apostle who should be emulated. When the rest of the disciples are afraid to go back to Judea because of the violent threats to Jesus, Thomas bravely proclaims, "Let us also go, that we may die with him" (John 11:16). A few chapters later, when Jesus is explaining his plans to prepare for them a place of future hope, Thomas is confused but boldly pushes forward to better understand his Rabbi: "Lord, we do not know where you are going. How can we know the way?" (John 14:5 ESV).

But the story of Thomas we most often tell is of the time after the resurrection when he refuses to believe the testimony of his friends. Thomas, worn down by grief and fear for his own life, has isolated himself and misses Jesus' first resurrection appearance to the rest of the disciples. When he hears word of it, he cannot believe it. He is the picture of skepticism. He needs proof.

When Jesus shows up again, Thomas is there. In his generosity, Jesus volunteers his own scars as proof of his power and abiding love. The doubting disciple sees through the haze of his sorrow and trauma to the reality of Christ's resurrected presence. "My Lord and my God!" was Thomas's response (John 20:28).

This exclamation may feel familiar and fitting to us. But biblical scholars note that it is perhaps the most definitive declaration of Christ's divinity that we hear from any of Jesus' disciples. New Testament scholar Donald Guthrie writes, "This marks the highest level of faith recorded in this Gospel."[3] In these five words is an entire world of theology, doctrine, allegiance, passion, and—most importantly—hope. This from a man who moments earlier had rejected the notion that resurrection was even possible.

There's a reason why the story of Thomas has captured our imaginations. We always love a character we can mock or deride. We look down our pious noses. "At least I'm not like him," we may say when deep down, we know we are just like him in every way. We feel superiority and camaraderie all at the same time. Thomas is achingly relatable. No one wants to be the doubter. Yet doubt we all do.

Some of us feel like we are forever on a downward slide from the mountaintop experience of knowing Jesus in our youth. How can a thing that seemed so clear and compelling to us when we were younger now feel so opaque and disorienting? Who could have guessed that journeying with God would include so many shadowed valleys? Who could have known the life of faith would require so much…faith?

I don't remember too much about the moment I supposedly became a Christian. I am told I was three years old and that I came crying to my poor mother, who was trying to take a shower. My sister had apparently just told me all about an awful place called hell, had warned me that I would go there if I didn't invite a nice man named Jesus into my heart. My gracious mother threw on a robe, put her hair up in a towel, and scooped me up into her lap. She rocked me in our squeaky old blue recliner, soothed me until I prayed (of my own accord) a childlike prayer of salvation. I don't remember the words I said. But I do remember the softness of my mom's robe, the squeaking of the chair, and the triumphant face of my sister, who had just won her first convert.

Much sharper in my mind are memories from high school youth group, where I learned about the difference between positional sanctification and progressive sanctification. My youth pastor Brian wasn't content to just let us eat pizza and play dodgeball. He was determined that none of us should grow up to be theological lightweights. That meant come Wednesday night, we all showed up to youth group with Bibles, notebooks, and pens in hand, ready to rock out to Audio Adrenaline, and then study some atonement theory, eschatology, and ecclesiology. Brian taught in a way that was real, engaging, and empathetic to our hardest questions. That was a gift I've carried with me my whole life.

Brian told us that when it comes to our *position* before God, the Bible insists the believer is sealed in Christ. We are seen as righteous because of the righteousness of Jesus. There is nothing we must do to earn goodness or curry favor. When it comes to our *status*, we are sanctified.

But learning to *act* as a sanctified saint happens gradually over time as we discover how to walk in the ways of God and live out the call of Christlikeness. There are many different theological perspectives on how exactly this progressive sanctification plays out. Pentecostals emphasize the need for a baptism of the Holy Spirit.

The "Higher Life" view posits that we receive a "second blessing" when we "let go and let God" and fully surrender our lives to the Lord. Reformed theology notes that all true followers of Jesus *are*, in fact, always being sanctified, though some believers may give in to fleshly desires from time to time. John Wesley taught that it was possible to reach a state of "Christian perfection" in this life where the believer no longer willfully sins. Some schools of thought have implored Christians to acknowledge the lordship of Jesus if they want to progress in godliness. And there are varying perspectives on who exactly is most responsible for our sanctification: God or us.[4]

I didn't really understand the ins and outs of how exactly this was all going to work out. I just knew that I was supposed to be getting *better*. Holier. More and more like Jesus. I remember at some point along the way a pastor or maybe a Bible professor drawing a line graph of my sanctification process with a Sharpie on one of those giant white flip charts. The bottom left corner represented me in my sinful state before I asked Jesus to be my Savior. From there, a thick, straight line representing my increasing righteousness advanced upward toward the top right corner of the graph. That corner was heaven. Someday I'd get there, to that perfect, sinless state.

That clean, uncomplicated graph, drawn hastily on a lousy flip chart, set my expectations of what the Christian life would look like from that day forward. I knew my sanctification would be slow. But I thought it would be steady. I envisioned an uninterrupted incline. As that line rose, so would my piety, my goodness, my peace of mind, my happiness. I would end my life holier than when I started. Day by day, I would chronologically improve. Isn't that what all those theologians meant by "progression"?

But I have been surprised to learn that much of my Christian life has felt like a long *regression*. Or perhaps like a jagged or serrated line. By this, I don't mean that I started out as a straitlaced Puritan and ended up a drug dealer or serial killer. I just mean that there are many times in my life when I don't feel even close to Christlikeness, when all the wisdom I've accumulated over the last thirty-five years of walking with Jesus seems to fall by the wayside. My devoutness is often interrupted. There are many times when God feels far away.

The valleys of my spiritual life have all looked different. Some are more dramatic than others—like gorges or sinkholes. There are times when I've struggled with fear and anxiety. I've worried about the future, about what people think of me. This fear has led me to make bad decisions, to choose effort and striving over trust and rest. Other times I've allowed unwise habits to encroach upon my time, let mindless entertainment or bad company get the better of me. There are seasons when my default language is harsh belittlement and ungracious judgment. I've wielded my words to prove points that weren't important—to make my husband, friends, colleagues, or Twitter adversary feel small. I've resented others for excelling more than me. I've told half-truths to save my reputation.

But the valleys I know best are the ones that are simply overshadowed with doubt. These are the valleys where certainty is in short supply. They are marked by a distinct lack of God's presence, or at least his *felt* presence. These are the times when I've been strictly faithful to my quiet times, when I've been active in church, when I've sought the Lord in both praise and prayer and still, he feels absent, aloof, unknowable. The Holy Spirit seems uninterested in guiding my steps, in helping me make decisions, in soothing my pain. I feel unmoored. I am the living example of the doubter described in James 1:6: "The one who doubts is like a wave of the sea, blown and tossed by the wind." The intimacy with God I was promised was achingly missing.

Despite my sister's vivid description thirty-five years ago, I'm still not sure I'm theologically clear on all the specifics of hell. But I know there are moments when doubt sure does feel like hell. And the question I keep asking myself is this: Can my faith sustain my doubt? Or is doubt like what the poet Alfred, Lord Tennyson, described?

It is the little rift within the lute,
That by and by will make the music mute,
And ever widening slowly silences all.[5]

If there is one phrase that captures the zeitgeist of the era of evangelicalism I grew up in, it's this: "Christianity is not a religion. It's a relationship."

This is another one of those sentiments whose origins are a bit fuzzy. But, like the "God-shaped hole," it has been making the rounds among church folks for decades and has profoundly influenced how we think about our experiences of faith.

In the mid-twentieth century, renowned Swiss theologian Karl Barth critiqued the performative nature of religion in his magnum opus *Church Dogmatics*, describing it as the effort of man to save himself rather than rely on the grace of God.[6] As early as 1913, a Presbyterian mission leader named Robert E. Speer wrote, "The idea of religion as a body of information, as a method to be pursued in ethical behavior, is...nowhere found in the New

Testament. Christianity is not a religion in that sense at all. It is a living and personal relationship."[7] Somewhere along the way, the idea was shortened to the simple catchphrase we all know today. The Jesus People movement of the 1960s and 1970s may have been the first to popularize it, and everyone from Billy Graham to Jerry Jenkins to Rick Warren has used it to make a point in a sermon or book.

I'd dare not offer a critique of Barth's analysis of religion or of Pascal's "God-shaped hole." These men were brilliant thinkers who gave us volumes and volumes of theological insights. But we live in an age where sound bites do more to form us spiritually than the thoughtful, robust treatises of centuries past. We don't have the time for complexity or the patience for nuance. Christians have reduced and repurposed these ideas to fit our market-driven, quip culture. I'm afraid it's done more harm than good.

I certainly see merit in the admonition that faith cannot simply be robotic rule-keeping, performative rituals, or scholastic inculcation. The very real and deep intimacy that we can experience with God is something to be celebrated. I believe it was hard won at the cross and that the gift of the Holy Spirit is priceless. Our unhindered access to him no matter who we are or what we've done is nothing short of astounding.

But for me, the danger of seeing Christianity as a relationship *over* a religion was that I began to understand faith more as a feeling rather than a practice. The maxim led me to believe that faithfulness was primarily a felt affection and excitement for the Lord. It was all about my one-on-one emotional connection with Jesus. Institutional practices like rituals, sacraments, liturgies, and corporate confessions were seen as rote, redundant, performative, and cold. The experience of actually being *with* Jesus, of knowing him intimately through personal prayer and daily quiet time, was where faith really came alive. At least that's what I thought.

But we err grievously when we emphasize the individualistic *experience* of faith over the communal *practice* of faith. Faith is not primarily a feeling. It is an act of choosing, an undertaking of obedience. When a relationship with God is predominantly associated with sentiment, then when the positive, warm feelings are replaced by negative, cold feelings, we are led to believe our faith is faltering. In fact, it is in the moments of emotional disconnect that our faith does precisely what it is designed to do: choose God even when he feels far off.

Conservative Christians denigrate the "DIY" spirituality of the "nones"—those who claim no religious identity. But the evangelical emphasis of relationship over religion has "do it yourself" written all over it. It is individualistic in nature, and it should come as no surprise that it's taken off in a culture as self-obsessed as ours. In youth group and college, I remember worship leaders instructing us to draw an imaginary circle around ourselves as we began to sing. "Pretend it's just you and God in the room right now." They'd turn the lights out and the volume up so I couldn't see or hear anyone else around me.

All this relational, individualized language gave me the impression that faith is an exclusive, private love affair with God. And when that relationship fails to deliver on the hoped-for satisfaction, the solution, too often, is to walk away. I know there are a myriad of contributing factors at play when it comes to the mass exodus of young people from the Church. But I'm afraid that our church leaders, in an attempt to win our hearts for Jesus, oversold the feeling and undersold the framework. Individual connection was more important than communal commitment. Maybe the reason we think we can go it alone is because we were essentially told all along that we could.

Christianity was never meant to be a DIY project of spiritual or relational gratification. It is not some nebulous, esoteric undertaking of self-improvement or self-fulfillment. Christianity is indeed a religion. It can't be separated from its most fundamental creeds. It is a set of beliefs rooted in time, space, and most notably in a historic person who lived and breathed and walked the earth two thousand years ago. Like every religion, it comes with an ethic. It invites us to a specific way of life, taught by Jesus and undertaken by a group of women and men whose lives were changed by what they witnessed in him. Christianity's rituals and traditions matter because they bind us to something bigger than ourselves, affix us to the countless believers who have gone before us, saints from across cultures and centuries. Liturgical practices serve to operationalize holy habits into our daily rhythms and act as a divine safety net when we as individuals fail to emotionally connect with God.

The truth is, Christianity is a religion *and* a relationship. That is the marvel! If the thought of committing ourselves to a religion sounds like a drag, then we have no idea what a gift a deeply rooted, ritualized, habitual, communal faith can be!

When James admonishes his readers to pray without doubt, he is not thinking of doubt as merely a feeling. He is not simply referencing questions or fears that an individual may face. Rather, commentators believe he is talking about people who can't seem to make up their minds about who or what to commit to. It is a warning against equivocation, about wavering loyalties and hedging bets.[8]

Faith is a shared endeavor. James opens his epistle by proclaiming that the testing of our faith produces endurance. It was not uncommon in the Greco-Roman world to view the testing of virtue as something that strengthened the character and built moral stamina. "James, however, speaks not of the virtue of an individual but of a community's faith," writes New Testament scholar Luke Timothy Johnson. "Endurance is not the demonstration of an individual's moral character but of a community's fidelity to God as its source of being and worth."[9] The doubter, for James, is the double-minded person who knows the grace God has offered the community of faith, but who also wants to secure himself in the comforts and security of the world. The double-minded is the one who would avoid suffering at all costs, who wants to jump ship and leave his comrades behind when the seas get rough.

It was in his isolation that Thomas was overcome by unbelief. His story is one of renewed faith but not because he found it within himself to summon his courage and rouse his convictions. Instead, his friends testified to the resurrection and Thomas showed up to see if he, too, might bear witness to the impossible. Jesus' resurrection was an astounding miracle. But the miracle that makes my jaw drop every time I read the story is that Jesus graciously *found* Thomas, sought him out, offered his scars as proof before Thomas could even ask. "Peace be with you," Jesus said (John 20:26). The entire scene is a picture of wholeness. Peace with God. Peace with one another. Peace with oneself.

Jesus' Sermon on the Mount begins with a redefinition of what it means to live a happy life. While most of us would probably tag photos of a new home, a beautiful meal, a smiling kid, a successful ministry event, a weight loss goal reached, or a beach vacation with the hashtag #blessed, Jesus has other ideas. Blessing, he says, comes from being poor in spirit. According to Jesus, you are blessed when you grieve, when you are insulted, when you are persecuted. You are blessed when you are starving for righteousness, when you are thirsty for a right relationship with God.

How do we come to a place where we say that grief or want or ache is good? It has taken time and lots of unlearning, but I have experienced the beauty that is to be found in hunger and thirst. I have come to see that doubt can be a gift. It reminds me that I am no spiritual giant, that I cannot always manufacture saintly passion or zeal. I cannot fill up my own cup. My spirit is indeed poor, my soul meek. We must meet the end of ourselves sometimes. It is only then that we know the true, yearning intimacy of God's absence.

I think it's true what they say: "Absence makes the heart grow fonder." Perhaps the journey of knowing God is sometimes *not* knowing him. What I mean is, to ache for him in his absence is to know he is real and that his presence is necessary for our very breath. The longing for his presence—the search for his presence—this is part of the way we actually *experience* his presence. No one knows how much they love and crave water until they go a day without it. Perhaps it is the same with God. It is in my moments of doubt that my love for him has grown the most. I've realized how much I need him.

There are plenty of days that I miss my certainty. I am deeply homesick for it. But I can also say that my doubt has not been wasted. And in this way, perhaps that erratic and broken line has been steadier than I thought. My process of sanctification has not been straight, but it has also not been a free fall. Perhaps every dip in the journey, every break in the line has not hindered the climb after all. I am moving toward God. Or rather, like Jesus moving toward Thomas, God is moving toward me.

The emotional prosperity gospel leads us to believe that it is our stalwart certainty, upbeat attitude, and positive feelings that make Christianity appealing to the outside world. It was Karl Marx who said that religion is the opium of the masses. Let's not prove him right. Christianity *is* a demanding and serious religion. It invites us into a story that is filled not only with triumph but with pain. To commit to a religion as mysterious as ours is no small undertaking. Our faith is a blessed hope, but it is not always a cure-all. We evangelize the world not by parading our emotional prosperity but by confessing our desperation for him. We must not hide our brokenness. I believe our desperate yearning for him is the most compelling apologetic we can offer the world.

Daniel Taylor writes in *The Myth of Certainty*:

> Normally doubt is seen as sapping faith's strength. Why not the reverse? Where there is doubt, faith has its reason for being. Do I doubt when I look at the pain in the world...? Fine, this gives tested faith (not blind wishful thinking) a place to operate...Doubt makes its claims, even daily, and they are respected, but they do not determine the character of my life.[10]

What do I want the character of my life to be? I want it to be one of obedience, a "Yes, and amen—let it be so!" to the call and the promises of God. Sometimes, that amen is fervent. Sometimes, it is feeble. I take comfort in the fact that the Gospels regularly lift up the seekers who were deemed spiritually unfit by the theological elites of the day. They were people with sharp questions and raw pain. They were people who acted in faith even when they lacked certainty. An "unclean" woman who had been bleeding for years broke all the Levitical rules and reached out to touch Jesus hoping he would heal her (see Luke 8:43–48). A reviled Syrophoenician woman who was shooed away by the disciples begged for healing for her daughter: "Even the dogs eat the crumbs that fall from their master's table," she cried (Matt. 15:27). The wretched thief hanging next to Jesus on the cross realized with awe the sacrificial suffering of the Messiah, and in a last-ditch effort to taste grace pleaded, "Jesus, remember me when you come into your kingdom" (Luke 23:42). In all these instances, it was a bold *act* fueled not by sanctimonious intention but rather by a primal desperation that led to a true encounter with Jesus. These were people who were *hungry* for God.

I am afraid of flying. Airplanes, in my opinion, are objectively terrifying. This fear was certainly inconvenient for my career as an international aid worker. Every time I'd prepare for a trip, I'd run through all the statistics about how unlikely it is to perish in a plane crash. I'd review all the safety protocols that are now in place. While other travelers sipped coffee and munched on Cinnabon, I'd be the one standing at the terminal window, my nose pressed against the glass, watching the maintenance workers complete their inspections. I read somewhere that more people are killed annually by donkeys than in aviation accidents. But all of this did little to set my mind at ease. There's something about the concept of flying that is totally horrifying to me. Hurtling through the air at almost

600 miles an hour 35,000 feet above the ground in a cramped, metal, cylindrical tube is just not natural. It's not normal.

But my dad always reminds me that the most important thing is not to be free of apprehension. The crucial question is this: Did I get on the plane, or did I stay in the terminal? The choice is not *to fear or not to fear*. The choice is to either give up or voluntarily walk onto that awful contraption, find my seat, buckle up, and submit to the ride. When it comes to air travel, whether or not I feel at peace about it, I put my well-reasoned trust in it. I align my action with what I know to be prudent and probably true.

When Dad talks to me about flying, he isn't really talking about flying. He's talking about faith. And I love him for it.

"Faith is not a superpower. It's not a capacity for magical thinking, not a bent toward otherworldly positivity," writes author Jen Pollock Michel in her book *A Habit Called Faith*.[11] Faith is indeed a habit, a communal practice of saying yes and amen even when we are scared. In the same way that I am swept up in the din and hum of a busy airport, surrounded by passengers who, though irritable, seem confident their plane isn't going down, the "great cloud of witnesses" and the communion of saints summon me to get onboard, trust my gut, and strap myself in.

I wonder if the reason Christianity is so difficult sometimes is because it calls us to follow and trust in a God who died. A God who upended all our expectations of him. The Jewish people of Jesus' day wanted a triumphant God who would accomplish all their political goals and rout their enemies. Proponents of the prosperity gospel want a God who will make them healthy and wealthy. *I* want a God who will make me feel good, happy, and blessed. I want a God who gives me the desires of my heart, who will build *my* kingdom and make me comfortable. Sometimes, we must *allow* Christ to be crucified. It is only when God dies, or at least our expectation of him dies, that he resurrects again into our lives in a way that leads us to exclaim, as Thomas did, "My Lord and my God!"

Do not fear your lack. Do not fear your doubt. The hungry know that there is abundance even in the table scraps. The sick know that even the hem holds great power if it is the hem of God. The weak know that there is strength in the remnants, the margins, the odds and ends. The thirsty know that water lies only at the bottom of the well. The doubter knows that to touch the scars of his pain even just once is as much proof of resurrection as a parading host of radiant angels—that the vast reach of a tree, both of root and branch, first lives in the smallness of a seed. There is holiness even in the relic of a faith reborn. And it is worth the arduous, uphill climb to behold the tiniest scrap of bone that maybe, just maybe, is a miracle.

A BLESSING:
Hope

We know that the whole creation has been groaning as in the pains of childbirth right up to the present time. Not only so, but we ourselves, who have the firstfruits of the Spirit, groan inwardly as we wait eagerly for our adoption to sonship, the redemption of our bodies. For in this hope we were saved. But hope that is seen is no hope at all. Who hopes for what they already have? But if we hope for what we do not yet have, we wait for it patiently.

—Romans 8:22–25

I once heard that the earliest Christians refused to plant gardens. Apparently, they were wholly convinced that Jesus would be coming back within a matter of weeks or months. They didn't see the point of investing in a garden. They assumed the coming kingdom made all agricultural endeavors pointless and trivial. These early followers of Jesus would often greet one another by exclaiming, "Maranatha!" a word that meant "Come, Lord." And they believed he would come quickly.

Two thousand years later, here we are. Still waiting.

We live in a world that pushes us toward unflinching optimism and positivity. In the face of failure, loss, and doubt, we are told to keep our chins up, to think happy thoughts, and to keep our eyes peeled for silver linings. As I've wrestled with my disappointment with the Church, as I've floundered in my grief, and as I've stumbled along on my journey of faith, I've found that this cheery idealism has been broken again and again. But it has been replaced by something more clear-eyed and true, something more sustainable than syrupy sentimentality or wishful thinking. My fragile idealism has been replaced by a sturdy, grounded hope.

Proverbs 13:12 says, "Hope deferred makes the heart sick." Since Christians have been waiting millennia for the return of their Savior, it would be a safe bet to say we are a heartsick lot. But if you step into most church services or Christian bookstores across this country, you'll see very little evidence of that inward groaning Paul writes of in Romans. You'll struggle to find the disillusioned words of Qohelet hand-lettered on reclaimed barnwood. "Meaningless! Meaningless!…Utterly meaningless! Everything is meaningless" (Eccles. 1:2) makes for terrible home decor. The Christian culture, eager to sell itself to the world, is much more comfortable with proud displays of victory, peace, and positivity.

But the virtue I would like to see people of faith recover is the virtue of honesty. Of authenticity. Yes, we are the people of "Maranatha!" But we are also the people of "How long, Lord?" We are people whose hearts are set on waiting. The Christian life is by nature a life of lament. We are bearers of a great light. But we are also the night watchmen.

We may think we are people who have found the secret to filling that God-shaped hole in our hearts. But we live with another void, another cavern of unmet desire that the secular world may never fully experience. Through Jesus, we've seen what righteousness and justice actually look like. Being a person of hope means we live with an abiding frustration with how things *are* because we are keenly aware of exactly how things *should be*. Sometimes, being people of hope means living with a righteous indignation—at injustice, at oppression, at abuse. We are people of anticipation, of longing, of eagerness. We are people of the wilderness, of exile.

Hope sings at a vastly different frequency than optimism. It eclipses the toxic positivity so prevalent in today's culture. Optimism can tell us tiny but attractive lies: *Everything's fine; you'll get over it; things could be worse; time heals all wounds.* Hope, instead, tells the whole story. It names the darkness. It embraces heartbreak. It looks death square in the face. But it also points us to love. It offers the possibility of survival. It directs us toward wholeness and resurrection. While it brings an airiness and levity to our lives, hope is also somber. It is serious. Hope is an anchor and line, heavy and taut.

The difference between optimism and hope is sometimes the difference between fiction and nonfiction. I think this is why hope has stood the test of time. Hope speaks truth. It has a way of harmonizing lament with praise. It allows sorrow and joy to coexist, to befriend one another.

This right relationship between sorrow and joy, this *peace*, this true shalom allows us to proceed into the world as people of peace. It means that our frustration, anger, and sadness are not channeled into more acts of harm. Rather, they are channeled into acts of service and justice that confront the evil all around us. Ours is a well-informed, well-equipped resistance against the curse—well informed because we know the truth of what could be, and well equipped because the Spirit moves with us, granting us the fruit of God's presence as we act in response to this holy unhappiness.

C. S. Lewis once said that hope is a theological virtue.[1] If virtues are to be embodied, then hope is to be *lived* as much as it is *believed*. Writes author and professor of philosophy James K. A. Smith, "Learning virtue—becoming virtuous—is more like practicing scales on the piano than learning music theory: the goal is, in a sense, for your *fingers* to learn the scales so they can then play 'naturally,' as it were. Learning here isn't just information acquisition; it's more like inscribing something into the very fiber of your being."[2]

Hope is a habit, a way of living. It is more than simply believing in your head that everything is going to be okay. It is *acting* as if these heirlooms of truth, handed down by generations of Christians who came before us, are indeed true. What, exactly, is this hope we hold? Good *will* overcome evil. Love *will* overcome hate. Joy *will* overcome suffering in the end. Sin has not forever destroyed our relationship with God and with one another. We have been restored.

These things are true.

I *hope* these things are true.

As believers, we are often reminded of how frequently the Bible commands us to "fear not," and to "be anxious for nothing." Fear and anxiety are thought to be the result of fickle faith, the by-product of a bad theology. Despite my theological rigor, I've struggled mightily to coax my fears into subsiding. Anxiety is persistent, innovative, sly.

Lately, it has helped me to think of fear and hope less as thoughts that live in my mind and more as actions that live in my body. Fear, I think, will always occupy space in my brain, but it doesn't have to animate my hands, my feet, or my mouth. And hope must do more than enliven my thoughts. It must set my body in motion.

I don't think God is angry at us for our concerns or our sadness. Professional counselor and author Krispin Mayfield suggests seeing those scriptural admonitions to "fear not" in the same way you would view a parent comforting their frightened child.[3] When my daughter cries for me in the night because she is afraid of the monsters outside her window, I tell her not to be afraid. It is not a reprimand or a rebuke, but rather a consolation, a reassurance that she is safe in our home, that the monsters, at least most of them, are not real.

While God is patient with our fear, I do think he entreats us to not despair. This is not a severe imperative, as if we are in danger of the fire of hell if fear sometimes gets the better of us. No, it is an invitation, a kind, steady hand reaching out to us as if to say: *Trust me. All is not lost.* The beautiful proposition of hope is our truest, purest calling.

The apostle Paul wrote often of this calling. He knew that tolerance for a long wait is part of the Christian life. Hope both requires and inspires patience. Hope is often paired with the concept of endurance in Paul's epistles. In 1 Thessalonians 1:3, he writes to his fellow believers, "We remember before our God and Father your work produced by faith, your labor prompted by love, and your endurance inspired by hope in our Lord Jesus Christ." In a modern-day culture where most of our discomforts are quickly and easily remedied, many of us have lost our capacity to wait. "Patience is mastery of our own discomfort—and it's a superpower," writes author and journalist Helen Russell.[4]

Endurance is a tall order because it's easy to get stuck in a moment. Sorrow or unmet desire can feel like a small dark room with no doors or windows. It's hard to see the way out, to feel like there is any future beyond the present you are trapped in. Sometimes the "now" feels like it is all there is.

Hope has a way of expanding our vision, of helping us see our pain in light of a larger context. Hope widens our view, pulls us out of the dark room and up to a higher place to really get the lay of the land. It situates our sorrow within a bigger story, puts the address of our pain on a larger map. Jen Pollock Michel says it's helpful to think of life with a long view of things—like the slow work of geological formation:

> Somehow that feels deeply biblical to me—considering our time geologically. It's the sanity of saying that we aren't as important as we think, that our lives are a wisp in the winds that bluster their way toward eternity, that we will be measured not by the incremental use of our minutes but by the architecture of our years. Geological timing helps the big things recover their proportion…It also allows the little things to shrink to their proper stature.[5]

It helps me to remember my own story in this way. I'll always be tempted to take a myopic view of my daily heartaches, spiritual lapses, or disappointments in the Church. But one day is *not* an eternity, no matter how much it may feel that way. Perhaps we'd do well to take at least one cue from the ancient Greeks, who took a long view of life, measured its goodness only at the very end when all aspects could be weighed on the scales. Did we persevere through the difficult days and years with virtue and patience? If we give ourselves long enough, if we don't rush the process, then we can trust that things will change. We can grow. So can the Church. What we are weathering today will eventually carve a beautiful landscape into all the tomorrows.

AFTERWORD

D oes God want me to be happy?

If you've made it this far through the book, this may be a question you are asking yourself, and I don't blame you. I've been asking myself that question for a long time too.

"God is more concerned with your holiness than your happiness." The first time I heard this well-worn statement preached from the pulpit, I found it to be strangely comforting. I was glad to know that any pain I was experiencing in life was accomplishing a noble end: the refinement of my character so that I could stand before God as good and acceptable. He needed to make me righteous—even if that meant afflicting me with loss or sorrow—so that he could tolerate me. I scribbled the phrase down in my notebook and whispered it through tears for years to come.

As I've taken great pains to point out in this book, these catchy phrases can sometimes have an inordinate amount of influence on how we think of the life of faith. I don't disagree with the idea that God wants us to be holy. But I'm afraid we've created a false dichotomy. If God is most concerned with my holiness, then does that mean my happiness doesn't matter to him at all? Do holiness and happiness stand in opposition to one another? Why can't God be concerned with both my holiness *and* my happiness?

Hedonism. Virtue. Fortune. Divine reciprocity.

Philosophers have always had a lot to say about happiness. So does the Bible. Happiness in Scripture is often framed around the concept of blessedness. The Old Testament word for "blessed" is *baruk*. When applied to God, it has a sense of praise, but when applied to people, it suggests a state of contentment or well-being. Ancient followers of God believed that blessing was a direct result of obedience to God and his laws. They clung to a venerated and time-tested formula: If I am good, God will be good to me.

Theologian and songwriter Michael Card notes that while the people of Israel held tightly to the notion that Torah obedience would always lead to blessing, Scripture reveals many exceptions to the revered rule. Suffering often rears its ugly head in the lives of the most God-fearing Old Testament heroes, and obedience does not always amount to ease or prosperity. Moreover, God sometimes chooses to bless people who live outside his Torah commandments, something David complains about many times in the Psalms. Job is a story in which we see the formula completely inversed—a righteous man laid low precisely *because* he was righteous. The ancient hypothesis is blown to bits again and again, and so, we often find the people of God wailing in lament and confusion.[1]

And we lament too. When our "if this, then that" assurances fail to deliver—when a job, a marriage, a ministry, or a community doesn't provide the happiness we hoped for—we feel lost. The ancient Israelites were probably tempted to see God in the same way we do—as a means to an end. Whether it be material or emotional, we leverage our good behavior for prosperity. We leverage a good relationship with God for abundance.

It shouldn't be this way. Whenever our commitment to a blueprint or formula exceeds our commitment to God himself, life will feel broken. I don't believe God ever wanted obedience to the Law to be a down payment for happiness. He wants intimacy with us, a true relationship. He wants to be near us. In Leviticus 26:12, God tells the people that if they follow his commands, "I will walk among you and be your God, and you will be my people." As my dad likes to say, God is not the means to an end. He *is* the end.

In the New Testament we find a new word for the concept of blessedness, the Greek word *makarios*. Jesus often uses this word in a way that undermines our typical understanding of prosperity. According to Jesus, the poor are considered blessed. So are the persecuted, the oppressed, the childless, and the hungry.[2] These seeming deficiencies are, in the end, what lead us into the kingdom, what fill us up and help us see the divine. The Beatitudes are a picture of intimacy with God.

Indeed, Christianity is not a story of transaction. It is a story of struggle. And a struggle is intimate. It requires closeness, honesty, and vulnerability. It involves risk. Christianity is not an apparatus of abundance or a contractual agreement with God that ensures he will give you everything you ever wanted. Christianity is a covenant, a binding of oneself to God and to his ways not as a service rendered for payment, but as a response to an invitation of love.

"You are always with me, and everything I have is yours," the father said to the older, beleaguered son (Luke 15:31). God's greatest aim is to be near us, to be Immanuel, God with us. The same God who chose to tabernacle among his people wants to live in our hearts. His presence is how he intends to bless us. His presence is not a means to some other emotional end. His presence *is* the end. It is the goodness, it is the happiness, and it is the deepest reality of a blessed life.

Ce_r

So then. Does life with God make us happy? What good is the presence of God in our lives if it doesn't always *feel* like peace or *feel* like intimacy? I've circled around and around this question again and again as I've written this book. I've wrestled with it, lost sleep over it, cried over it, almost gave up on this book because of it.

My guess is that if you were to ask people today why they participate in religion or in spiritual practices, many would say because these things make them *feel* good. Faith or spirituality creates a sense of emotional centering. It brings them peace.

I may be wrong, but I have come to believe that this good feeling cannot be the reason we choose to follow Jesus. I absolutely agree that peace and joy and courage are often a beautiful by-product of a deep walk with God. Studies confirm that religious habits do, in fact, positively impact a person's mental health.[3] But I just no longer believe that faith is a means to a therapeutic end, or that God is simply a mechanism by which we achieve self-actualization. I don't really think that true religion is primarily a method of personal or emotional transcendence. It is not merely a security blanket or soothing salve. When we make it that, it will always disappoint us.

Faith, as I now understand it, is simply the heart's response to something it recognizes as true. Faith is saying yes to something that is right, and good, and holy. I now think of Christianity as a path or a road. It is a manner of walking. It is a way of being, not just a way of thinking. In fact, I have come to believe that it is *the* Way. It is *the* Truth. And we walk this way of God *with* God. His presence is good because it illuminates the path and helps the world to make sense somehow.

Yes, the Bible does gives us a Law to live by. But it was never meant to be used as a bargaining chip; that's not how the Law was designed. The book of Proverbs is filled with instructions on how to live a godly life and includes descriptions of the consequences of choosing good or evil. But Proverbs is not really a list of divine reciprocities, or a book of guarantees—"if this, then *always* that." Rather, it should be seen as a collection of conventional wisdom that, when applied, generally leads us to goodness, justice, and thriving relationships.[4] Good decisions do not always lead to the fulfillment of our every desire. But a life lived in God's presence is a pilgrimage toward wholeness, toward right relationship with ourselves, with others, and with God. Wise choices create an environment that is conducive to flourishing. As the Old Testament book of Deuteronomy reminds us over and over again, follow the Lord's commands "so that it may go well with you."

The areas of life I've covered in this book are not inherently unhappy. Work, marriage, parenting, and community are not bad. They've just been mythologized. Their rewards have been rushed and their ease exaggerated. "It will go well with you," but sometimes, it will take time. Again, like the ancient Greeks said, the "goodness" of one's life may only be accurately assessed at the end, when you can audit the overall trajectory of your days and see the abiding character of your hours and weeks and years.

In writing this book, I've come to realize how beautiful the Way of Jesus really is. Call it an ethic. Call it a moral code. All I know is that it is an incredible gift to be provided with values and habits that serve as a compass on the sometimes strenuous, sometimes meandering journey of life. We will always be litigating the many details of this ethic, what is and is not harmonious with the heart of God. But there are some fundamental ways of living that I have seen rise to the surface again and again as I've researched and written this book. It is an ancient ethic that, while countercultural even today, was almost unheard of in the societies in which Christianity first emerged:

Staying humble.

Serving the poor.

Having compassion for both neighbor *and* enemy.

Honoring the image of God in oneself and others.

Making and keeping promises.

None of these values are easy. Living them out comes with a cost. But God's presence, I believe, makes these values possible, enables us to embrace them. Of course, there will be difficult times, deep losses, and painful emotions. Some stretches of this road are truly hard. But I believe the path is ultimately good, the destination worth the trek.

The Hebrew word *asher*, which means "happy" or "blessed," is believed by some scholars to be derived from a root word that means "to go" or "to go straight."[5] This suggests action or movement. The Jewish culture of Jesus' time made a deep connection between belief and behaviors. For them, theology was to be embodied if it was truly believed. *Torah*, the name given to the first five books of the Hebrew Scriptures, literally means "instruction," and Jewish sources note that the root word likely means "to throw or shoot an arrow." The picture is of an arrow moving straight and true.[6]

Faith is not euphoria. But ours is a faith that walks. Breathes. Moves. The very first Christians were often referred to as people belonging to "the Way." Jesus was serious when he said this road was narrow and the gate to get there was small. Few people, indeed, ever find it. But I believe they are the happy few, the blessed few.

The people I know who are the happiest are indeed walking on this narrow way. Happiness, in their lives, is less about a feeling in the moment and more about movement over the course of a lifetime. They are people who are content with their limits. They sacrifice themselves, but they don't intentionally martyr themselves. There is no sense of self-aggrandizing or performance. They serve simply from a place of love. They laugh easily. They are more likely to be found looking up at the sky rather than down at their phones. They notice good things, sweet things. They don't seem to take themselves too seriously. Their minds are preoccupied with others more than with themselves. They are patient. They are not prone to panic. They have made peace with their pain and allow themselves to be sad when hard times come. For them, happiness looks like right relationship with God, right relationship with others, and right relationship with themselves.

Perhaps it's best to strike a healthy balance between the ancient Greek philosophers and the New Thought mesmerists of the late 1800s. The power of positive thinking cannot thwart every tragedy that comes our way. But we *do* have at least some agency over how we respond to hardship and suffering.

While writing this book, I've made it my mission to try to practice what I've preached. If I have suggested that unhappiness can indeed be holy, then I've tried to live as if it really is. Whenever I've experienced an unhappiness of some kind, rather than stuff it down, ignore it, or judge it as unholy, I've brought it out into the light. I've given myself permission to feel it.

The result has been rather surprising. When I found myself willing to experience difficult emotions, my courage actually increased. When I stopped seeing happiness and positive feelings as a commodity that I had to scrimp and save, I started making better choices. I was able to simply *be* in the sorrow. I had more clarity when my vision wasn't clouded by fear of adversity. It didn't feel like optimism, but it felt like soundness of mind. I became more willing to have hard and necessary conversations with people. I was more eager to serve in ways that stretched me. Strangely, I also became more willing to embrace my limits because I wasn't afraid of the difficult feelings that others would have when I said no.

Developing a tolerance for hard feelings also allowed me to better assess my actions in light of the reality of personal sin and failure. Permitting myself to feel shame when I'd hurt someone or made a harmful choice did an important work in me. While it did not define me or change the value I had in Christ, holy conviction, though painful, motivated me to make important changes in my habits and behaviors. As Paul writes in 2 Corinthians 7:10–11:

> Godly sorrow brings repentance that leads to salvation and leaves no regret, but worldly sorrow brings death. See what this godly sorrow has produced in you: what earnestness, what eagerness to clear yourselves, what indignation, what alarm, what longing, what concern, what readiness to see justice done.

When I allow my heart to stretch—to expand to accommodate hard emotions—then it doesn't burst when hard times come.

AFTERWORD

The pain doesn't shatter me, and the anger doesn't explode. When
sadness or disappointment is not the great, looming enemy, then,
suddenly, spats within marriage shrink to an appropriate size.
A hard day at work doesn't prompt me to hurriedly turn in my
notice. I am able to process my grief more wholly and healthily
because I'm not trying to avoid it. I'm willing to stay present in
an uncomfortable conversation or situation longer, especially if I
know the effort will yield wholeness in the long run. Good fruit is
made possible by patience. Patience is made possible by a willingness to be in pain, at least for a time.

So many caveats are needed here. We are not commanded to
remain in abusive situations, or to forever pour ourselves out simply to placate someone else. We are not to be exploited or manipu-
lated. And submitting ourselves to unnecessary suffering because
we think it will somehow please God or make us holy is not at all
what I am speaking about here.

I'm simply recognizing that the idolization of happiness is no
way to live. Life itself calls us to hard and painful things. The ability to accept this and endure has made this world such a better
home for me. I'm not always trying to vacate my hurting heart or
brace to protect myself from difficulty. I am no longer numb. I can
enjoy the ride, summon my courage to face what comes, and stick
with the things that truly matter to me in the long run.

While the pursuit of Christ is indeed a narrow way, a specific
path to walk, so is the rigorous pursuit of happiness. I've spent far
too long squeezing my life into a narrow understanding of what
it meant to be blessed, plagued by the impossible expectation of
perfect bliss. Happiness is a tyrant, demanding all our attention
and all our allegiance. When idolized, it sucks the life out of our
relationships, our ministries, and our families.

God is not a means to an end. Neither are our spouses, our kids, our friends, our jobs, or our churches. When we are willing to accept that not all of life exists to bring us personal fulfillment, it opens up a wide space in our hearts, allows us to say yes to all that life brings us, to say yes to good things that are beautiful *and* hard.

I still believe in the title of this book, that unhappiness can be holy. The word "holy"—in Hebrew *qodesh* or *qadosh* and in Greek *hagios*—simply means "to be set apart." It especially denotes that something or someone has been set apart for a divine purpose.[7] There is an incredible amount of purpose in our pain, not exactly in a utilitarian sense, as if suffering is the ultimate optimizer or enhancer. I just believe unhappiness serves the purpose of illuminating our lives, of offering wisdom and clarity. Sometimes unhappiness is the heart's way of telling us that something is wrong, something needs tending. Sometimes it is life's way of telling us our expectations were unrealistic. Sometimes it is God's way of reminding us of what is true and good, of what *could* and *should* be. Sometimes it is life's way of showing us that what we labored toward was weighty and depleting and absolutely worth it.

For as long as I can remember, I'd embraced the myth that my life had to always *feel* good, *feel* rewarding, and *feel* meaningful in order to be blessed. I was a faithful disciple of the emotional prosperity gospel. But I have come to believe that to simply exist as a beloved child of God, to see him and to live, to wrestle with him and know that he is always with me, *this* is the great gift. *This* is the Way. It is enough. As Frederick Buechner wrote, "Listen to your life. See it for the fathomless mystery that it is. In the boredom and pain of it no less than in the excitement and gladness: touch, taste, smell your way to the holy and hidden heart of it because in the last analysis all moments are key moments, and life itself is grace."[8]

$$Ce\gamma$$

I began this book by describing a persistent and perplexing sadness that felt like a stone in my shoe. Unfortunately, I have to tell you that I'm afraid that stone is here to stay.

I wrote earlier of our philosopher friend Blaise Pascal. Pascal, the conceptual architect of the "God-shaped hole," was a Christian who was said to have had an encounter with God one night that was so powerful, he kept a written account of it stitched in his jacket pocket. Despite that mountaintop experience, he was realistic about the challenges of a walk with God. He believed that to exist as a human was, by design, to know an unavoidable restlessness.

Pascal observed that we all struggle to sit alone in our idleness, in stillness and silence. We are always striving, chasing after something: more money, more love, more accomplishments, more happiness. Our experiences are never enough; there is always something around the next corner, always something to pursue. We cannot be still, Pascal posits, because stillness forces us to grapple with the excruciating reality of suffering and death. We cannot cope with our own precariousness, our own mortality.

According to Pascal, human beings are beings of disproportion. By this he means that we are *thinking, feeling* beings, the only creatures on earth who can really conceptualize eternity, meaning, morality, and the universe. And yet, we are as fragile as any other living thing. We are as delicate and fleeting as the grass of the field. "Man infinitely transcends man," Pascal famously concludes in the *Pensées*.[9] Put another way by philosopher Benjamin Storey, "To be human is to feel like a deposed king, a man dislodged from his rightful place."[10] Deep down, we know that we were made for more.

I can think of no truth more biblical than this. Since our departure from the Garden of Eden, the curse has separated us from the original intent of our creation. We have eternity in our hearts— as the wise sage notes in Ecclesiastes 3:11—and yet we are finite in our strength, we don't know all the answers, and our flesh is mortal. Our souls long for what *should* be, while our bodies live in the hard reality of what is. Suddenly, Pascal's image of the God-shaped hole makes a lot more sense. Only, in Pascal's mind, it is impossible to fill that hole this side of eternity. Pascal joins a chorus of other God-fearing voices—Augustine, Aquinas, Qohelet—who name, essentially, the same dilemma. Whether for our sin or our fragility or our unrealized aspirations, it is difficult—if not impossible—to achieve happiness in this life.

The emotional prosperity gospel will always seek to minimize the curse. But sadness is the human condition. Restlessness is an appropriate response to what's been broken. It is not an aberration that can be corrected. Whether your pain is a boulder or a pebble in your shoe—it is holy, as holy as any moment of happiness you may experience. If you struggle with disappointment, frustration, or anticipation, it is not because you are inadequate or spiritually immature. It is because you are a human living in the aftermath of the fall. Existence will always feel like an incomplete sentence, like a hunger never fully satisfied.

Pascal would posit that we achieve pure happiness only when we fully enter the presence of God in the life after life, the resurrection, the coming kingdom of Christ. "Our heart is restless until it rests in you,"[11] wrote Saint Augustine in his *Confessions*. Yet Augustine also wrote with conviction that this *rest* is rarely found in the here and now: "As long as [man] is in this mortal body, he is a pilgrim in a foreign land, away from God."[12]

I wrote this book because it was the book I needed. And I suppose this may seem like a somber, unhappy way to end it. If you picked up this book because you thought it was the book *you* needed, then I sincerely hope you are not disappointed in this conclusion. I'm aware that books with sad endings sometimes struggle to sell, and readers would often prefer happy payoffs and easily applied takeaways. It is no wonder the genre of self-help is so popular.

But my guess is that you, like me, are not looking for a quick fix for your sadness. You aren't looking for a new formula for prosperity or a ten-step plan. You are looking for some points of light for the journey. You are just trying to find some footing on this narrow path. And if that is the case, then my prayer is that you would find true blessing beneath all the layers of optimism, beyond our meager understanding of prosperity and abundance: delight in the ordinary, humility in your efforts, hope even in sadness. I believe God's presence makes these blessings possible. And my prayer for *us* is that we would realize that real joy isn't a thing to be chased. Joy is what we get when we are chasing the right thing. In the words of an old Puritan prayer:

When thou art absent all sorrows are here,
When thou art present all blessings are mine.[13]

ACKNOWLEDGMENTS

I'm incredibly thankful to my team at Worthy and Hachette, including Daisy Hutton, Cat Hoort, and Laini Brown. Beth Adams, you have been more than an editor. You have been a guide, advocate, encourager, and friend. To my agent, Rachelle Gardner, thank you for the ways you have walked beside me in my writing journey.

I'm grateful to the Asir family and the Chinta family. I was forever changed by your kindness, welcoming spirits, and open arms. Becky Sumrall, thank you for taking me under your wing when I was young, eager, and a bit self-important. I'll always be grateful that I learned the day in and day out of ministry under your wise and gentle shepherding. Thank you also to my former colleagues at Samaritan's Purse for showing me what it means to engage in the difficult and beautiful work of serving.

I am so very thankful to our church family at the Heart. Witnessing your deep faithfulness to Christ has been one of the most formative experiences of my life.

I've received such generous encouragement from other writers along the way, including K. J. Ramsey, Jen Pollock Michel, Lore Wilbert, Kendall Vanderslice, Kimberly Stuart, Anneli Matheson,

Daniel Gleason, Catherine Parks, Jeff Chu, and Sarah Bessey. I'm grateful. Big shout-out to my songwriting circle here in Boone— thanks for keeping me rooted and for consistently bringing the creative goods. As always, thank you, Kelly Sites, for the prayers.

It's humbling to admit how much help I needed with this book. For the folks who read portions or early drafts of this manuscript—including Rachel Lonas, Justin Lonas, Ethan Hardin, Brian Hilliker, Alison Wicker, Anna Grace Glaize, Marla Decubellis, Lizzy Aitken, Graham Aitken, Joni Byker, Katie Hagaman, and Michael Sheldon—words don't adequately express how grateful I am to you for your insights and feedback. I don't know how I ended up with so many brilliant and kind friends, but I am so thankful.

Taylor Hardin, your intuition, keen eye, and companionship as a fellow writer—plus your willingness to hang out with my kids—helped me see this book through to the finish line. Thank you.

I'm grateful to the LaPlue family, the Evans family, and the entire Opelt family. Amy and Eddie, I'm glad we were quarantined together so that you could talk through so much of the content of this book with me. Thank you for listening. Dennis and Jean—this book would never have been written without you. You've shouldered so much for us over the last few years, and I'm so thankful for your constant help and encouragement.

Mom and Dad, thank you for creating a childhood environment for me and Rachel that allowed us to challenge the norms, pursue our questions, and wrestle with doubt. You showed us a faith that was kind and safe to come home to. That has made all the difference.

Lois and Jane, thank you for bringing so much laughter and fun into our lives. Being your mom is a gift from God.

Finally, Tim. Thank you. You are a man who has always cared more to *be* than to *seem*. Thank you for all the seen and unseen ways you make this life of ours so, so blessed. You have *always* done the needful.

NOTES

Introduction

1. Ross Douthat, *Bad Religion: How We Became a Nation of Heretics* (New York: Free Press, 2012), 184.
2. Kate Bowler, *Blessed: A History of the American Prosperity Gospel* (New York: Oxford University Press, 2013), 61, 91.
3. Douthat, *Bad Religion*, 188.
4. Darrin M. McMahon, *Happiness: A History* (New York: Grove Press, 2006), 9.
5. Clark Lawlor, *From Melancholia to Prozac: A History of Depression* (Oxford: Oxford University Press, 2012), 25.
6. McMahon, *Happiness*, 3, 11.
7. Ed Ayers, Brian Balogh, Nathan Connolly, and Joanne Freeman, hosts, "The Pursuit: A History of Happiness," July 29, 2016, on *BackStory*, podcast, https://podcasts.apple.com/us/podcast/backstory/id281261324?i =1000371759414.
8. Helen Russell, *How to Be Sad: Everything I've Learned About Getting Happier by Being Sad* (New York: HarperOne, 2021), 15.
9. Bowler, *Blessed*, 226.
10. Jeff Reimer, "Holiness in the Virtue & Vice Tradition: An Introduction to the Seven Deadly Sins," Eighth Day Institute, accessed October 31, 2022, https://www.eighthdayinstitute.org/holiness-in-the-virtue-vice-tradition.

Chapter 1: Work

1. Alex Derr, "Mountain Climbing Quotes," *The Next Summit*, January 8, 2022, https://thenextsummit.org/mountain-climbing-quotes/.
2. John Bergsma, "The Creation Narratives and the Original Unity of Work and Worship in the Human Vocation," in *Work: Theological Foundations and Practical Implications*, ed. R. Keith Loftin and Trey Dimsdale (London: SCM Press, 2018), 12.

3. Catherine L. McDowell, *The Image of God in the Garden of Eden* (Winona Lake, IN: Eisenbrauns, 2015), 199.

4. Darrell T. Cosden, "Work and the New Creation," in Loftin and Dimsdale, *Work*, 171–72.

5. John H. Walton, *The Lost World of Adam and Eve: Genesis 2–3 and the Human Origins Debate* (Downers Grove, IL: InterVarsity Press, 2015), 105–6.

6. Lisa Sharon Harper, *The Very Good Gospel: How Everything Wrong Can Be Made Right* (New York: WaterBrook, 2016), 13.

7. Bureau of Labor Statistics, https://www.bls.gov/news.release/tenure.nr0 .htm.

8. Edward Baptist, "The Industrial Revolution," February 21, 2014, in *American Capitalism: A History*, podcast, https://podcasts.apple.com/us /podcast/american-capitalism-a-history/id826726603?i=1000263306863.

9. James Steuart, *An Inquiry into the Principles of Political Economy*, bk. 1 (London, 1767), chap. 7, 40, quoted in Jan de Vries, *The Industrious Revolution: Consumer Behavior and the Household Economy, 1650 to the Present* (New York: Cambridge University Press, 2008), 67.

10. Haydn Shaw, *Generational IQ: Christianity Isn't Dying, Millennials Aren't the Problem, and the Future Is Bright* (Carol Stream, IL: Tyndale, 2015), 48.

11. Shaw, *Generational IQ*, 46.

12. Jefferson Bethke, *To Hell with the Hustle: Reclaiming Your Life in an Overworked, Overspent, and Overconnected World* (Nashville: Nelson Books, 2019), xiv.

13. Bruce Tulgan, *Not Everyone Gets a Trophy: How to Manage the Millennials* (Hoboken, NJ: Wiley, 2016), 10.

14. John H. Walton, *The NIV Application Commentary* (Grand Rapids, MI: Zondervan, 2001), 229.

15. Jay Wesley Richards, "Be Fruitful and Multiply: Work and Anthropology," in Loftin and Dimsdale, *Work*, 117.

16. Timothy Keller, *Every Good Endeavor: Connecting Your Work to God's Work* (New York: Penguin Books, 2012), 90.

17. David Fagerberg, quoted in Bergsma, "Creation Narratives and the Original Unity," 18.

Chapter 2: Marriage

1. Stephanie Coontz, *Marriage, a History: How Love Conquered Marriage* (New York: Penguin Books, 2006), 24–43.

2. Coontz, *Marriage*, 10.

3. Coontz, *Marriage*, 16–18.

4. Beth Allison Barr, *The Making of Biblical Womanhood: How the Subjugation of Women Became Gospel Truth* (Grand Rapids, MI: Brazos Press, 2021), 108.

5. Coontz, *Marriage*, 134.

6. Coontz, *Marriage*, 148–50.

7. Coontz, *Marriage*, 156.

8. Coontz, *Marriage*, 164.

9. Coontz, *Marriage*, 180.

10. Coontz, *Marriage*, 226.

11. Coontz, *Marriage*, 232.

12. "U.S. Nuns on the Decline as Fewer and Fewer Women Take Up Religious Orders," Religion News Service, *Huffington Post*, October 14, 2014, https://www.huffpost.com/entry/us-nuns-decline_n_5982888.

13. Edward Cody, "A Language by Women, for Women," *Washington Post*, February 24, 2004, https://www.washingtonpost.com/archive/politics /2004/02/24/a-language-by-women-for-women/a0083923-539b-4182 -b809-d11090f787df/.

14. J. M. S. Pearce, "Before Charcot," in *Hysteria: The Rise of an Enigma*, ed. J. Bogousslavsky (Basel: Karger, 2014), 2.

15. MaryB. Safrit, host, "Normalizing Christian Singleness (feat. Katelyn Beaty)," December 20, 2022, *Unsuitable with MaryB. Safrit*, podcast, https://podcasts.apple.com/us/podcast/normalizing-christian-singleness-feat -katelyn-beaty/id1440164058?i=1000590734904 .

16. Katie Gaddini, "A Large Number of Single Women Are Leaving the Church. Why?" *Relevant*, November 4, 2021, https://relevantmagazine .com/faith/church/why-are-so-many-single-women-are-leaving-the-church/.

17. Katelyn Beaty, "Joshua Harris and the Sexual Prosperity Gospel," Religion News Service, July 26, 2019, https://religionnews.com/2019/07/26/joshua -harris-and-the-sexual-prosperity-gospel/.

18. "The Trends Redefining Romance Today," Barna Group, February 9, 2017, https://www.barna.com/research/trends-redefining-romance-today/.

19. "The Best Winnie the Pooh Friendship Quotes," *Southern Living*, June 6, 2022, https://www.southernliving.com/culture/friendship-quotes-winne -the-pooh.

20. C. S. Lewis, *The Four Loves* (New York: Harcourt, Brace, and World, 1960), 87.

21. Robert D. Putnam, *Bowling Alone: The Collapse and Revival of American Community* (New York: Simon & Schuster, 2000).

22. "The Return of the Multi-Generational Family Household," Pew Research, March 18, 2010, https://www.pewresearch.org/social-trends/2010/03/18/the-return-of-the-multi-generational-family-household/.

23. Skye Jethani, Kaitlyn Schiess, Christian Taylor, and Phil Vischer, hosts, "Episode 432: The Idol of Individualism with E. Randolph Richards," November 25, 2020, *Holy Post*, podcast, https://podcasts.apple.com/us/podcast/the-holy-post/id591157388?i=1000500256057.

24. W. B. Yeats, *The Collected Poems of W.B. Yeats*, ed. Richard J. Finneran (New York: Scribner, 1996), 80–81.

25. Yeats, *Collected Poems*, 81.

Chapter 3: Parenthood

1. Terence E. Fretheim, commentary ed., *The New Interpreter's Bible*, vol. 1 (Nashville: Abingdon, 1994), 364.

2. Martin Luther, "To Several Nuns: From Wittenberg, 6 August 1524," from *Briefe aus dem Jahre 1524 No. 733–756* (Letters of the Year 1524, Nos. 733–756), Weimarer Ausgabe, trans. Erika Bullmann Flores, https://www.projectwittenberg.org/pub/resources/text/wittenberg/luther/nuns.txt.

3. Walter J. Chantry, "The High Calling of Motherhood," Reformed Reader, accessed November 11, 2022, http://www.reformedreader.org/rbb/chantry/motherhood.htm.

4. Stephen West, "Episode 4 Plato," July 1, 2013, in *Philosophize This!*, podcast, https://podcasts.apple.com/us/podcast/philosophize-this/id659155419?i=1000162005901.

5. Kevin DeYoung, "It's Time for a New Culture War Strategy," Gospel Coalition, June 17, 2020, https://www.thegospelcoalition.org/blogs/kevin-deyoung/its-time-for-a-new-culture-war-strategy/.

6. Coontz, *Marriage*, 155, 164.

7. Quoted in Russell, *How to Be Sad*, 120.

8. Anne Morrow Lindbergh, *Gift from the Sea*, 50th anniversary ed. (New York: Pantheon Books, 2006), 23.

9. I'm grateful to Taylor Hardin for her wonderful insights on motherhood that contributed so significantly to my thought process on this.

10. N. T. Wright, "Women's Service in the Church: The Biblical Basis," paper for the symposium "Men, Women and the Church," St John's College, Durham, September 4, 2004, https://ntwrightpage.com/2016/07/12/womens-service-in-the-church-the-biblical-basis/.

11. Skye Jethani, Kaitlyn Schiess, Christian Taylor, and Phil Vischer, hosts, "Episode 543: Women and the Gender of God with Amy Peeler," January 11, 2023, *Holy Post*, podcast, https://podcasts.apple.com/us/podcast/the -holy-post/id591157388?i=1000595201651.

A Blessing: Delight

1. Kate Bowler, *Everything Happens for a Reason and Other Lies I've Loved* (New York: Random House, 2019), 156.
2. Justo L. Gonzáles, *A Brief History of Sunday: From the New Testament to the New Creation* (Grand Rapids, MI: Eerdmans, 2017), ebook.
3. Cole Arthur Riley, *This Here Flesh: Spirituality, Liberation, and the Stories That Make Us* (New York: Convergent, 2022), 31.

Chapter 4: Calling

1. Bruce Waltke, *Finding the Will of God: A Pagan Notion?* (Vancouver: Regent College, 1995), 22–40.
2. S.H.A.P.E. Test, https://www.freeshapetest.com/.
3. Stuart Jeffries, "Why Too Much Choice Is Stressing Us Out," *Guardian*, October 21, 2015, https://www.theguardian.com/lifeandstyle/2015/oct/21 /choice-stressing-us-out-dating-partners-monopolies.
4. Jeffries, "Too Much Choice."
5. Barry Schwartz, "The Paradox of Choice," July 2005, TED video, retrieved from https://www.ted.com/talks/barry_schwartz_the_paradox_of_choice /up-next.
6. Rhonda Byrne, *The Secret* (New York: Atria Books, 2006), 92.
7. Elizabeth Gilbert, *Eat, Pray, Love: One Woman's Search for Everything Across India, Italy and Indonesia* (New York: Penguin, 2006), 260.
8. Jen Sincero, *You Are a Badass: How to Stop Doubting Your Greatness and Start Living an Awesome Life* (Philadelphia: Running Press, 2013), 50.
9. Rhonda Byrne, *The Power* (New York: Atria Books, 2010).
10. Timothy Ferriss, *The 4-Hour Workweek: Escape 9–5, Live Anywhere, and Join the New Rich* (New York: Crown, 2007), 51.
11. Ferriss, *4-Hour Workweek*, 51.
12. Lauren Landry, "Tory Burch to Babson Graduates: 'If It Doesn't Scare You, You're Not Dreaming Big Enough,'" Business Journals, May 18, 2014, https://www.bizjournals.com/boston/inno/stories/news/2014/05/18/tory -burch-to-babson-graduates-if-it-doesn-t-scare.html.
13. John Eldredge, *Wild at Heart Field Manual: A Personal Guide to Discovering the Secret of Your Masculine Soul* (Nashville: Thomas Nelson, 2002), 16.
14. Eldredge, *Wild at Heart Field Manual*, 2.

15. Donald Miller, *A Million Miles in a Thousand Years: How I Learned to Live a Better Story* (Nashville: Thomas Nelson, 2011), 155.
16. Rachel Hollis, *Girl, Wash Your Face: Stop Believing the Lies About Who You Are So You Can Become Who You Were Meant to Be* (Nashville: Nelson Books, 2018), 5.
17. Stephen West, "Episode 22: Blast off to the Renaissance!" July 1, 2013, in *Philosophize This!*, podcast, https://podcasts.apple.com/us/podcast/philosophize-this/id659155419?i=1000312571712.
18. Giovanni Pico della Mirandola, *Oration on the Dignity of Man*, in *The Renaissance Philosophy of Man*, ed. Ernst Cassirer, Paul Oskar Kristeller, and John Herman Randall (Chicago: University of Chicago Press, 1948), 224–25, quoted in Norman Melchert, *The Great Conversation: A Historical Introduction to Philosophy* (California City, CA: Mayfield, 1995), 306.
19. Charles Taylor, *The Ethics of Authenticity* (Cambridge: Harvard University Press, 1991), 26.
20. Alan Noble, *You Are Not Your Own: Belonging to God in an Inhuman World* (Downers Grove, IL: InterVarsity Press, 2021), 22.
21. Michael F. Steger, Shigehiro Oishi, and Todd B. Kashdan, "Meaning in Life Across the Life Span: Levels and Correlates of Meaning in Life from Emerging Adulthood to Older Adulthood," *Journal of Positive Psychology* 4, no. 1 (2009): 43–52, cited by David B. Feldman in "The Paradoxical Secret to Finding Meaning in Life," *Psychology Today*, May 18, 2018, https://www.psychologytoday.com/us/blog/supersurvivors/201805/the-paradoxical-secret-finding-meaning-in-life.
22. Jesse Singal, "For 80 Years, Young Americans Have Been Getting More Anxious and Depressed, and No One Is Quite Sure Why," The Cut, March 13, 2016, https://www.thecut.com/2016/03/for-80-years-young-americans-have-been-getting-more-anxious-and-depressed.html.
23. Barry Schwartz, *The Paradox of Choice: Why More Is Less* (New York: Ecco, 2014), 208.
24. Shaw, *Generational IQ*, 48.
25. J. D. Douglas, organizing ed., *The New Bible Dictionary* (Grand Rapids, MI: Eerdmans, 1962), 180–81.

Chapter 5: Community

1. Thanks to Dan Enarson for offering this insight on the story of the good Samaritan.
2. Michael Card, *The Parable of Joy: Reflections on the Wisdom of the Book of John* (Nashville: Thomas Nelson, 1995), 50.

NOTES

3. Douglas, *New Bible Dictionary*, 1132.
4. *Wiktionary: The Free Dictionary* (San Francisco: Wikimedia Foundation), https://en.wiktionary.org/wiki/community.
5. Skye Jethani, "The Evangelical Industrial Complex and the Rise of Celebrity Pastors (Pt. 1)," *Christianity Today*, February 20, 2012, https://www.christianitytoday.com/pastors/2012/february-online-only/evangelical-industrial-complex-rise-of-celebrity-pastors.html.
6. Bob Smietana, "Report: Megachurches Continue to Grow and Diversify, Steer Clear of Politics," Religion News Service, October 29, 2020, https://religionnews.com/2020/10/29/report-megachurches-continue-to-grow-and-diversity-steer-clear-of-politics/.
7. Charles G. Finney, "Measures to Promote Revivals," in *Lectures on Revivals of Religion* (New York: Fleming H. Revell, 1853), accessed August 1, 2022, https://ccel.org/ccel/finney/revivals/revivals.iii.xiv.html.
8. Jeanne Halgren Kilde, *When Church Became Theatre: The Transformation of Evangelical Architecture and Worship in Nineteenth-Century America* (Oxford: Oxford University Press, 2005), 197.
9. Kilde, *When Church Became Theatre*, 87.
10. Jemar Tisby, *The Color of Compromise: The Truth About the American Church's Complicity in Racism* (Grand Rapids, MI: Zondervan, 2019), 17.
11. Bob Smietana, *Reorganized Religion: The Reshaping of the American Church and Why It Matters* (New York: Worthy, 2022), ebook.
12. Martin Luther King Jr., *Meet the Press*, April 17, 1960, retrieved from YouTube, https://www.youtube.com/watch?v=1q881g1L_d8.
13. Skye Jethani, *The Divine Commodity: Discovering a Faith Beyond Consumer Christianity* (Grand Rapids, MI: Zondervan, 2013), ebook.
14. Neil Postman, *Amusing Ourselves to Death: Public Discourse in the Age of Show Business* (New York: Penguin, 1985), 121.
15. Christina Caron, "An Overlooked Cure for Loneliness," *New York Times*, December 21, 2021, https://www.nytimes.com/2021/12/21/well/mind/loneliness-volunteering.html.
16. Putnam, *Bowling Alone*, 368–82.
17. Putnam, *Bowling Alone*, 383–87.
18. Putnam, *Bowling Alone*, 23.
19. Putnam, *Bowling Alone*.
20. Dawn C. Carr, Ben Lennox Kail, Christina Matz-Costa, and Yochai Z Shavit, "Does Becoming a Volunteer Attenuate Loneliness Among Recently Widowed Older Adults?" *Journals of Gerontology* 73, no. 3 (March 2018): 501–10, https://doi.org/10.1093/geronb/gbx092.

21. González, *Brief History of Sunday*.
22. Justo L. González, *The Story of Christianity, Vol 1: The Early Church to the Dawn of the Reformation* (New York: HarperOne, 2010), 110.
23. Richard Swenson, *Margins: Restoring Emotional, Physical, Financial, and Time Reserves to Overloaded Lives* (Colorado Springs: NavPress, 2004), 94.

Chapter 6: Body

1. John W. Kleinig, *Wonderfully Made: A Protestant Theology of the Body* (Bellingham, WA: Lexham Press, 2021), ebook.
2. For the history of body image and Christianity, see R. Marie Griffith, *Born Again Bodies: Flesh and Spirit in American Christianity* (Los Angeles: University of California Press, 2004). For accounts of anti-Black theology within the American church, see Ibram X. Kendi, *Stamped from the Beginning: The Definitive History of Racist Ideas in America* (New York: Nation Books, 2016), 63–64.
3. Amy Kenny, *My Body Is Not a Prayer Request: Disability Justice in the Church* (Grand Rapids, MI: Brazos, 2022), ebook.
4. Kleinig, *Wonderfully Made*.
5. Peter Scazzero, *Emotionally Healthy Discipleship: Moving from Shallow Christianity to Deep Transformation* (Grand Rapids, MI: Zondervan, 2021), 96.
6. Esther Lombardi, "20 Most Famous Quotes from the Roman Poet Ovid," ThoughtCo., January 17, 2020, https://www.thoughtco.com/quotes-from -the-roman-poet-ovid-740996.
7. Wendell Berry, *The Art of the Commonplace: The Agrarian Essays of Wendell Berry*, ed. Norman Wirzba (Berkeley: Counterpoint, 2002), 118.
8. Daniel Jonce Evans, "Make Fix Build," blog, August 24, 2022, https:// danieljonce.com/.
9. Tom Fish, "12 Mind-Blowing Facts About Your Body," *Newsweek*, October 27, 2021, https://www.newsweek.com/mind-blowing-facts-about-your -body-human-1638872.

A Blessing: Humility

1. Scot McKnight, *The Story of God Bible Commentary: Sermon on the Mount*, ed. Tremper Longman III and Scot McKnight (Grand Rapids, MI: Zondervan, 2013), 156.
2. McKnight, *Story of God Bible Commentary*, 165.
3. Dallas Willard, *Renovation of the Heart: Putting on the Character of Christ* (Colorado Springs: NavPress, 2002), 18.

NOTES

4. Matthew 16:20, Mark 3:12, and Luke 8:56 are a few verses where we see the motif of the Messianic Secret.
5. C. S. Lewis, *The Weight of Glory* (Grand Rapids, MI: Zondervan, 2001), 34.
6. John Calvin, *A Harmony of the Gospels: Matthew, Mark and Luke*, trans. D. W. Torrance (Grand Rapids, MI: Eerdmans, 1972), 1:202, quoted in McKnight, *Story of God Bible Commentary*, 157.

Chapter 7: Sanctuary

1. "Signs of Decline and Hope Among Key Metrics of Faith," Barna, March 4, 2020, https://www.barna.com/research/changing-state-of-the-church/.
2. Douglas, *New Bible Dictionary*, 228, 229.
3. Origen, *Against Celsus*, 3.55, quoted in González, *Story of Christianity*, 60.
4. I'd like to thank Mike Sheldon for all his insights as I processed and wrote this chapter.
5. Thanks to Ethan Hardin, a student of Dr. Spencer's, who shared this concept with me.
6. John E. Hansan, "Settlement Houses: An Introduction," 2011, Social Welfare History Project, accessed October 10, 2022, https://socialwelfare .library.vcu.edu/settlement-houses/settlement-houses.
7. Thank you to my friend Graham Aitken for these thoughtful observations.
8. "2022 Global Scripture Access," Wycliff Global Alliance, September 1, 2022, https://www.wycliffe.net/resources/statistics/qa-2022-global -scripture-access/.
9. Barbra Mann Wall, "History of Hospitals," Penn Nursing, University of Pennsylvania, accessed October 6, 2021, https://www.nursing.upenn.edu /nhhc/nurses-institutions-caring/history-of-hospitals/.
10. "American Donor Trends," Barna, June 3, 2013, https://www.barna.com /research/american-donor-trends/.

Chapter 8: Suffering

1. Kathryn Reid, "2004 Indian Ocean Earthquake and Tsunami: Facts, FAQs, and How to Help," World Vision, December 26, 2019, https://www .worldvision.org/disaster-relief-news-stories/2004-indian-ocean-earthquake -tsunami-facts.
2. Ella Wheeler Wilcox, "Solitude," Poetry Foundation, https://www .poetryfoundation.org/poems/45937/solitude-56d225aad9924.
3. McMahon, *Happiness*, 473.
4. I'm grateful to Harry Mathis for our conversation this year that helped shed light on Aristotelian logic and how much it fails us in times of suffering.

NOTES

5. Joseph Henry Thayer, *Greek-English Lexicon*, accessed through BibleHub, https://biblehub.com/greek/1515.htm.
6. George Arthur Buttrick, commentary ed., *The Interpreter's Bible: The Holy Scriptures in the King James and Revised Standard Versions with General Articles and Introduction, Exegesis, Exposition for Each Book of the Bible* (New York: Abingdon-Cokesbury Press 1951), 280.
7. Barbara Brown Taylor, *Learning to Walk in the Dark: Because Sometimes God Shows Up at Night* (San Francisco: HarperOne, 2014), ebook.
8. Barbara Brown Taylor, "A Subsistence Spirituality," Evolving Faith Conference, Denver, Colorado, October 4, 2019.
9. Greg Sterling, "*Mors Philosophi*: The Death of Jesus in Luke," *Harvard Theological Review* 94, no. 4 (2001): 383–402, http://www.jstor.org/stable/3657414.
10. Douthat, *Bad Religion*, 11.
11. Nicholas Wolterstorff, *Lament for a Son* (Grand Rapids, MI: Eerdmans, 1987), 81, 91.

Chapter 9: Sanctification

1. Blaise Pascal, *Pensées: Section VII, Morality and Doctrine, 425* (New York: Open Road Integrated Media, 2011), accessed November 9, 2022, ProQuest Ebook Central.
2. Elaine Jordan, "The Legend of St. Thomas or 'Pai Sumé,'" Tradition in Action, October 7, 2017, https://www.traditioninaction.org/religious/h150_Tomas.htm.
3. Donald Guthrie, ed., *The New Bible Commentary* (Grand Rapids, MI: Eerdmans, 1970), 966.
4. Andy Naselli, "Models of Sanctification," Gospel Coalition, accessed September 29, 2022, https://www.thegospelcoalition.org/essay/models-of-sanctification/.
5. *English Poetry III: From Tennyson to Whitman*, vol. 42 of The Harvard Classics, ed. Charles W. Eliot (New York: P. F. Collier & Son, 1909–14; Bartleby.com, 2001), accessed November 20, 2022, www.bartleby.com/42/.
6. Karl Barth, *Church Dogmatics: Volume 1, Second Half-Volume* (Edinburgh: T. & T. Clark, 1956), 297–325.
7. Robert E. Speer, "Only the Name," *Record of Christian Works*, vol. 32, ed. and pub. W. R. Moody (1913), 559.
8. Gordon Poteat, contributor, *The Interpreter's Bible*, vol. 12 (Nashville: Abingdon Press, 1957), 24.

9. Luke Timothy Johnson, contributor, *The New Interpreter's Bible*, vol. 12 (Nashville: Abingdon Press, 1998), 187, 188.

10. Daniel Taylor, *The Myth of Certainty: The Reflective Christian and the Risk of Commitment* (Downers Grove: InterVarsity Press, 1986), 81.

11. Jen Pollock Michel, *A Habit Called Faith: 40 Days in the Bible to Find and Follow Jesus* (Grand Rapids, MI: Baker Books, 2021), 20.

A Blessing: Hope

1. Lewis, *Weight of Glory*, 107.

2. James K. A. Smith, *You Are What You Love: The Spiritual Power of Habit* (Grand Rapids, MI: Brazos, 2016), 18.

3. Krispin Mayfield, *Attached to God: A Practical Guide to Deeper Spiritual Experience* (Grand Rapids, MI: Zondervan, 2022), ebook.

4. Russell, *How to Be Sad*, 45.

5. Jen Pollock Michel, *Teach Us to Want: Longing, Ambition, and the Life of Faith* (Downers Grove: InterVarsity Press, 2014), 173.

Afterword

1. Michael Card, "Lamenting Is Worship! Part 1," YouTube, February 17, 2009, https://www.youtube.com/watch?v=Pr3mNGtxd-I&t=9s.

2. Douglas, *New Bible Dictionary*, 160.

3. Skye Jethani, Kaitlyn Schiess, Christian Taylor, and Phil Vischer, hosts, "Episode 537: The War Over Christmas Movies & Gen Z's Mental Health with Josh Packard," November 30, 2022, in *The Holy Post*, podcast, https://podcasts.apple.com/us/podcast/the-holy-post/id591157388?i=1000588121192.

4. Thanks again to Pastor Mike Sheldon for pointing this out to me!

5. McMahon, *Happiness*, 78.

6. "What Does 'Torah' Mean?," My Jewish Learning, accessed January 1, 2023, https://www.myjewishlearning.com/article/what-does-the-word-torah-mean/.

7. Douglas, *New Bible Dictionary*, 530.

8. Frederick Buechner, *Now and Then: A Memoir of Vocation* (New York: HarperCollins, 1983), 87.

9. Blaise Pascal, *Pensées: Section VII, Morality and Doctrine, 434*, accessed November 9, 2022, ProQuest Ebook Central.

10. Institute for Classical Education, "History of Happiness—Part 1/2 with Benjamin Storey," February 1, 2021, https://podcasts.apple.com/us/podcast/history-of-happiness-part-1-2-with-benjamin-storey/id1551378168?i=1000507356215.

NOTES

11. Augustine, *Confessions*, bk. 1, trans. Sarah Ruden (New York: Modern Library, 2018), 3.
12. Augustine, *City of God*, bk. 19, chap. 14, 873, quoted in McMahon, *Happiness*, 107.
13. Arthur Bennett, *The Valley of Vision: A Collection of Puritan Prayers and Devotions* (Edinburgh: Banner of Truth Trust, 1975), 55.